TRAVELING WITH GEORGE

An Out-of-This-World Experience

BETTY WALDRON PORTENLANGER

TRAFFORD
PUBLISHING

© Copyright 2006 Betty Waldron Portenlager.
All rights reserved. No part of this publication may be reproduced, stored in a retrieval system, or transmitted, in any form or by any means, electronic, mechanical, photocopying, recording, or otherwise, without the written prior permission of the author.

Cover design: Rachel McClain.

Note for Librarians: A cataloguing record for this book is available from Library and Archives Canada at www.collectionscanada.ca/amicus/index-e.html
ISBN 1-4120-5751-5

Printed in Victoria, BC, Canada. Printed on paper with minimum 30% recycled fibre. Trafford's print shop runs on "green energy" from solar, wind and other environmentally-friendly power sources.

Offices in Canada, USA, Ireland and UK

Book sales for North America and international:
Trafford Publishing, 6E–2333 Government St.,
Victoria, BC V8T 4P4 CANADA
phone 250 383 6864 (toll-free 1 888 232 4444)
fax 250 383 6804; email to orders@trafford.com
Book sales in Europe:
Trafford Publishing (UK) Limited, 9 Park End Street, 2nd Floor
Oxford, UK OX1 1HH UNITED KINGDOM
phone 44 (0)1865 722 113 (local rate 0845 230 9601)
facsimile 44 (0)1865 722 868; info.uk@trafford.com
Order online at:
trafford.com/05-0650

10 9 8 7 6 5 4 3

George Francis Portenlanger
(1942 – 2002)

*To George,
my invisible means of support*

ACKNOWLEDGEMENTS

The heavens have sent so many people to help me along the way. I need to thank them.

For obvious reasons, I first thank George.

Next, I thank my daughters, Kate and Margaret. Throughout this experience, we have cried and laughed together, and yelled and laughed some more.

To my mother, Ruth: what can I say, little Ruth? For my entire life, you have shown me an example of unbelievable strength.

To Carol Dirck, my bridge and my connection. You were truly heaven-sent.

To the following dear people who each, in his or her own supportive way, allowed me, and helped me to be:

Jeanine Belz
Maureen Esposito
Kathi Olson
Joan Power
Sue Belz
Kris Peterson
Alice Horn
Mary Coriglione
Charles McKeon
Beth Shanahan Elliott
Michelle Witczak
Donna Buti
Frances Motiwalla
Mike Ksiazek
Mary Grundy
Sue Lamb
Liz Brieva
Lee Snyder
Cyndi Lopardo

I love each and every one of you!

And, to all others not named, who gave me courage and strength, I sincerely thank you.

I owe special thanks to my editor, Robb Murray, who smoothed my writing into more readable form. Not only is he extremely capable and an expert at his craft, but he is compassionate, as well. I so much appreciate his help!

To Rachel McClain for her genuine interest in this project, her generous spirit and her gift of considerable talent in designing the cover. I will be forever grateful.

To Pat Longanecker, deep gratitude for taking the photo in Ireland that is included in this book. It is something I treasure. Her perfect timing and the circumstances surrounding the moment hold a deep meaning for me.

Finally, my deepest thanks—to my dear, dear friend, Lois Anderson, who gave me a safe place to cry, repair, renew and laugh again. Without her unlimited generosity—emotionally and spiritually—I shudder to think where I would be at this moment.

Her source of energy and support knows no bounds! Who else would have shared my instant recognition for the priceless value of a brass French-fry bucket?

George and I both thank you, Lois. I will never be able to repay your kindness and goodness. May you have blessings unending!

CONTENTS

Acknowledgements	7
Introduction *by Kathi Haller-Olson*	3
Introduction *by Lois Anderson*	5
Author's Foreword	6

PART ONE: THE BEGINNING		9
1	My Narrative Begins	11
2	His Endearing Ways	13
3	A Spiritual Man	17
4	Changing Residences—and a Sign	22
5	George's Final Four Days	25

PART TWO: THE END		29
6	The Crisis—in Slow Motion …	31
7	At the Hospital	35
8	Back at Home	40

PART THREE: HONORING THE DEPARTED		45
9	The 'Graduation to Heaven' Party	47
10	Grief = Fear	55
11	Side Effects / Affects of Death	58
12	Tributes and Consolation	62
13	Lois and Carol	73
14	Solo to Oahu	78
15	The Volcano of Kilauea	81
16	The Finale	89

PART FOUR: CONNECTING		95
17	For Your Consideration …	97
18	Connecting	98

PART FIVE: AN ONGOING PRESENCE	115
19 Ordinary Man, Extraordinary Soul	117
20 Orchestrating Beth and Betty	125
21 Just a Few More Stories, I Promise!	128
22 Some Dreams	131
23 Sharing George	136
24 Decoding the Gift	137
PART SIX: ACCEPTING THE PROCESS	139
25 Uncharted Waters	141
PART SEVEN: ADDENDA	147
26 Addenda	149
27 Afterword	151
APPENDIX: E-MAILING HEAVEN	155
28 E-Mailing Heaven	157
29 Messages to Repair a Broken Heart	163
30 The Final Communication	213
ABOUT THE AUTHOR	217

I have asked two very special friends to introduce this book. They graciously consented to do so. I treasure their words and their friendship.

INTRODUCTION
BY KATHI HALLER-OLSON

A minister once told me that "there are no coincidences" and that if we keep ourselves open we will see the connections between others and ourselves.

Therefore, I am sure it was no coincidence that I met Betty Waldron Portenlanger, in a hallway that was crowded with eager young women waiting to go to a rush party at Northern Illinois University.

She caught my eye because we were both attired for this auspicious event in the same sweater. A few words were exchanged—perhaps "Nice sweater!"—and then we were whisked off to the sorority house to be entertained.

Several nights later, on the occasion of being asked to be part of a sorority, I found myself once again in the company of the "sweater" girl. This was the beginning of a friendship that is now forty-plus years old, and still going strong.

Some years later, it was again no coincidence when I met George Portenlanger while he and Betty were on their first date. My husband and I were at a casual dinner place with college friends and were about to leave the restaurant when we spotted Betty and George. "They make a nice couple," I thought, and indeed, they did! As we came to know George, we knew that this was a marriage made in heaven: two soul mates who somehow found each other in this chaotic world. They shared, among other things, a crazy and wild sense of humor. We could always count on convulsing in laughter when they were around.

I could go on and on about all the times that Betty and I have called each other at just the precise moment that the other was thinking of doing the same, the times when we have been there to share the worst moments of our lives or the times when we have celebrated the best.

Since the time that George left this world so abruptly, Betty has discovered that he is still very much a presence in her life. The strong connection that they had on earth keeps them connected in some very interesting, sometimes bizarre, but always comforting ways.

It is not a coincidence that I have been asked to introduce this book that is at the heart of my friend's journey. It is an honor to help her on her way.

Richard Gillard composed these hymn lyrics (for "The Servants Song") that sum up our time spent together as friends:

> I will weep when you are weeping,
> When you laugh, I'll laugh with you.
> I will share your joy and sorrow
> 'til we've seen this journey thru.

INTRODUCTION
BY LOIS ANDERSON

Betty and George were wildly in love with life and each other. Their laughter, levity and love permeated their time together, and their home as well. Those of us lucky enough to spend time with them always left lighter for the experience.

We all wondered how such soul mates could be separated and survive without each other's support. Amazingly, but, somehow, not surprisingly, it became clear that these two would continue along the path together: Betty from Here, George from There.

What you hold in your hands is an amazing account of love being felt beyond death. Having witnessed many of these incredible events myself, there is no doubt in my mind that George—and many others who have departed this earth—can be heard, can be spoken to, and can be loved in previously unimagined, but very tangible, ways.

Gentle George ... quiet, quick-witted, kind, warm and welcoming George ... connecting with and through the Universe in ways no one could have imagined possible when he was alive. Fun and funny, spirited, full of laughter and of love and of life ... even now, years after his death, he continues to impact us with his sense of humor, his uncanny timing, and his wit and wisdom.

So here's to you, George: thank you for showing us, in no uncertain terms, that life does go on, that connections can be made and that communication can exist with those on the other side. Your death has given birth to hope for those of us who have already lost, or who will inevitably lose, someone we love ...

AUTHOR'S FOREWORD

The purpose of my writing has been threefold:

First, I needed to share my experiences regarding the George Portenlanger I knew and the one I continue to know;

Second, this was a cathartic exercise for me, a way of surviving the two years immediately following his death;

and,

Third, I wanted to tell a story, our story, of love and connecting—connecting then, and now, and for what I know will be forever.

From the moment that that incredible light went out in my life, I did not allow my mind to focus on myself and my emotional pain. Rather, I focused on the thought: Where did he go? From the beginning of the end, I tried to concentrate on figuring out what had happened to the vibrant energy that was known, in this lifetime, as George Francis Portenlanger.

George had a theory that we live in levels of wavelengths. *(Sorry, George. I'm not going to be able to do your thoughts justice, but I'll try.)* I now know that he was discussing the string, quantum, and parallel universe theories. Just as there are different bands on a radio, what if there are different bands in life energy? For now, we're only tuned to this "station," this frequency. On a radio, with a slight adjustment to the knob, you can go from weather, to rock, to shock, to religion, to all-news, to country & western, to oldies, to an almost unlimited variety — *ad infinitum*. If a radio can pick up this variety of transmissions, why can't it be a possibility that several scenes are also happening simultaneously in life?

George was intrigued with the idea that, if we could adjust our "dial," even ever so slightly, we would be able to tune in to hearing, seeing and experiencing a variety of channels that would revolutionize our way of knowing.

After his death I thought, "OK George, if your light has gone out on *my* level, *my* frequency, I will do my best to try to tune in to *your* expanded realm."

I realize that I have left myself open to ridicule because of my path. Some people may question my sanity, while others may be embarrassed for me because they feel I don't know that he is dead. I know he's dead. I knew it from the moment I stood in the street following the car accident. But dead to *what*? Only dead to life as we know and understand it, yet all the while trying, very forcefully, to get our attention, so that we can also share in the joyful discoveries of his present existence!

George, who from the time he was little had a difficult time being contained in his earthly body, is now soaring free. Soaring free and loving it! Meanwhile, I'm trying to adjust my dial so that I can tune in to him without any static. *(Come on George, give me a break. You know I'm technophobic and now I'm supposed to do what? This is way out of my league!)* But, I am finding it exciting and I do believe that I've made some breakthroughs in ways I never would have imagined.

I have gone from January, 2002, when I thought, "I'm not going to survive this," to January, 2004, when I realized that I *was* surviving.

It is a road that I never dreamed I would be traveling and a route I certainly never would have chosen.

Like the game show *Let's Make a Deal*: "Choose what's behind Door #1, Door #2, or Door #3." I don't remember choosing this door, but this is the door that opened and I was given the cruelest surprise of a lifetime.

My progress in healing has been made not because of anything I have or have not done. I am "making it" because of countless others. It has been solely with help that has so generously been given to me— help seen and unseen, help known and unknown. In experiencing all of it, I am totally humbled, totally amazed and totally grateful.

After George's death, someone who was remembering him commented that, while she loved him, there were times when "you just had to get away from him. He could overwhelm you with his talking and his ideas."

I replied, "He was the only one on this earth from whom I *never* wanted to get away."

He was the smartest, funniest, wittiest, wisest, kindest, most outrageous and most trustworthy person I have ever known.

God, how I loved him! God, how I still do!

Realizing that George would want me to keep enjoying life, I have tried to do just that. However, I wouldn't be able to go on if I didn't think there was a purpose to all that has happened. Actually, I still have no idea what that purpose may be. I only know that this is all for my benefit.

As a friend of mine, Kim Androw, wrote: "The Universe is benevolent and unfolding in your favor." I love that, and I truly believe it as well. This is quite a journey. This particular part of my life's journey is not of my choosing. I have, however, made the conscious choice to honor the experience.

So, there you have it. I wrote this story because I had to. May you read it knowing that it is George's true story of all-encompassing, unselfish love ... connected love ... past, present and future ...

Betty Waldron Portenlanger

PART ONE: THE BEGINNING

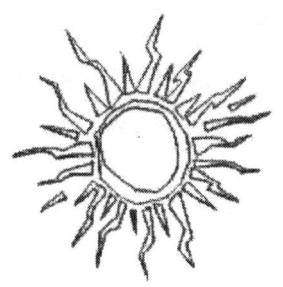

1 MY NARRATIVE BEGINS

When I first met George, he was wearing a Nehru jacket, a peace symbol on a leather cord and a huge red mustache.

I suppose I didn't look much better. I was wearing a red dress with white polka dots. Thinking back, the dress looked just like something Little Orphan Annie would wear.

It was October, 1968. He was 26 and I was 23.

I went home and told my father that some hippie was going to call and, when he did call, I wasn't going to be home.

George didn't call for a few days. My phone number was Rodney 3-8171. One had to dial the first two letters, RO, plus the number in order to reach me. But it turned out that George kept dialing R Operator (zero), plus the number, and repeatedly got a busy signal. After throwing away my number because he couldn't connect, he retrieved the paper, deciding to give it one more try. It must have been divine intervention because he then realized his mistake and dialed correctly.

Thinking that he would never call, and because it was prior to caller ID, I answered the phone when it rang. I never dreamed that it would be the "hippie."

"Would you like to go out?"

"Oh, thank you, I'd love to."

And the rest is history. The sequencing of our life together had begun.

We had met in October, 1968.
We were engaged in December 1968.
We were married in July 1969.

11

We were blessed with two daughters, Catherine Jean (Kate) and Margaret Ellen (Molly).

George used to comment that we had already been married for three months before our first year had gone by.

I would say, "We didn't know one another at all."

And he would say, "We knew one another, Betty."

How did he know? Of more importance, how could I not have known?

To describe to you the delightful soul named George Francis Portenlanger is almost impossible. Mere words don't do the animated version justice.

As his death notice read:

PORTENLANGER

George F. Portenlanger, 59, died Jan. 21, 2002. True love, best friend and unbelievably fantastic husband of Betty, nee Waldron; cherished and adored father of Catherine and Margaret; devoted son of the late Joseph and the late Cora Portenlanger; dear son-in-law of Ruth (the late Thomas) Waldron; dearest brother of Stephen (Kathryn), Joseph (Joanne), John (Joann), Rita (Abdul) Qaiyum and Mary (the late Dennis) Coriglione; beloved uncle of many nieces and nephews. United States Air Force Veteran, member I.B.E.W. Local #134. George was one of a kind, larger than life, a gentle man and a gentleman. He had a deep love for his family and possessed an amazing wealth of knowledge. He was a man of heart and wit. We will miss him immeasurably. Thank you, George. You were THE BEST! May the Heavens welcome you with open arms. Family and friends will be received at his home on Thursday, Jan. 24, from 1 until 9 p.m., in celebration of his unique and blessed life. Interment private.

2 HIS ENDEARING WAYS

The mini-snapshot provided by George's death notice pales in comparison to the real George.

For a fuller picture, let me tell you of the George who left me with a myriad of memories and stories. Here are some of the impressions/stories about him that I have always dearly loved:

♥ George, who, at the age of seven, had *rheumatic* fever, but really thought that he had suffered from *romantic* fever.

♥ George, who went to night school for eight years after we were married to earn an economics degree.

Upon graduation, his average was so high that he was invited to sit on the stage with the deans. Watching him walk down the aisle, talking non-stop to his processional partner, I was convinced that he wasn't paying attention to where he was actually supposed to sit.

"Oh no, he's going onto the stage!" I thought. I had had no idea that he was being honored.

In true Dear George fashion, he had forgotten to bring his name card that would help the speaker call on him when it was his turn to be announced. How delightful to watch him trying to explain the pronunciation of his last name, in a split second, to the presenter. Vintage George.

♥ George, who would give cooking tips to the little "older" ladies when he was doing electrical work in their homes. They not only trusted him to do fair, honest, excellent work, but also received culinary information at the same time.

♥ George, who would write a detailed thank-you note to one of my students, every holiday, when she gifted him with a treat bag. He would empty the contents onto the table so that he could enumerate each item. Carefully, he would print the note so that the child would be able to read it:

Dear Ashley,

Thank you for the two pieces of pink bubble gum, three chocolate hearts, one special pencil, one candy bar and four pieces of chewy candy.

Your friend,
Mr. Portenlanger

♥ George, who made darling *and* delicious heart shaped pizzas each Valentine's Day.

♥ George, who bought front row tickets each year for the Nutcracker Ballet.

When Margaret was six years old, her favorite part was the Snow Prince and the Snow Princess dancing together. That year, for about two weeks after seeing the performance, Margaret wore a white communion dress, and envisioned herself as the Princess. George, dressed in white long underwear, played the Prince. He would lift her high and they would "dance" and spin and twirl through the house. She was indeed a Princess and he was truly a Prince.

♥ George, who knew more facts and trivia than any other living soul and who would impart this knowledge whether or not it was requested. For example, "You can make four bullets from one tuna fish can." How did he know this? *Why* did he know this?

♥ George, who refinished all the wood in our 100-year-old home, including the beamed dining room ceiling.
One year, our home was selected to be on the neighborhood historical society Christmas House Tour. On the day of the tour, people began arriving, but George was nowhere to be found.
After spending almost the entire day greeting guests and listening to their positive exclamations about the beautiful wood and excellent restoration job, I went to find George. He was in the basement reading.
"George, you've got to come upstairs so that you can hear what everyone is saying about your great work."
"Do you like it, Betty?"
"You know I love it," I replied.
"Well, you're the one I did it for, and so, if you like it, that's all that matters."
Completely satisfied, he went back to his reading.

♥ George, who would repeatedly run/jog around the block or the park attired in jeans, plaid shirt, Irish cap and blue Nikes.
One year he entered the Thanksgiving Turkey Trot, a run held to help some special cause. He was dressed in his usual running gear. You should have seen everyone else, dressed in their spandex, looking at him, and thinking, "This dude is going to run in *that*?"
He did. He didn't win, but finished with his personal best time.

♥ George, who answered the phone at 2:30 AM one morning

and, in a high pitched voice that he thought sounded exactly like Kate's, told the teenaged boy on the other end that it was "too late, too late" to call.

I was in the background yelling "What are you doing? Hang up the phone!"

Apparently, his imitation of Kate was quite authentic. I had the irate mother routine down to a science.

Never again was our sleep interrupted. What a team!

(I wrote the above paragraph while in Hawaii. At the time, it was almost midnight, and I was alone in the condo. As I was writing about the phone incident, the phone rang. I answered it, but the phone kept ringing in the receiver and then went dead.

It was extremely strange, but I smiled as I hung up the phone and said, "Hi, George. That was pretty good. How did you do that? I love you and I thank you.")

A SPIRITUAL MAN

George was a big man in all ways: physically (tall, but not heavy), emotionally, intellectually and spiritually.

He had a heart of gold and some of his grief experiences would be too painful to describe in full. It would be impossible, for example, to relate the difficult, transitional events of taking our dog, Fluffy, to the Orphans of the Storm Animal Shelter, bringing his beautiful German Shepard, Maxine, to the vet at the end of her life, or experiencing the demise of Cootzer, our cat of twenty years.

His kindness to animals was surpassed only by his kindness to people. His father, suffering from Parkinson's, was in a nursing home during his last days. George and I had gone to visit him one evening and found his father peacefully sleeping. When we were leaving the room, I will never forget watching George bend down to kiss the dear man on his forehead, stroke his hair, and softly say, "*Gute Nacht, Papa. Schlaf' wohl.*" (Good night, Papa. Sleep well.) It was something that he had heard his German-born father say to him each night as a child. As George turned toward me, a tear was running down his cheek. His father died the next day.

Everyone has a favorite George story. Tales of and about him could go on forever. He was an interesting, delightful personality, raised by two understanding and wonderfully loving parents, Joe and Cora Portenlanger. The third of six children, George had three brothers and two sisters:

Stephen
Joe
(George)
John
Rita
Mary

Growing up in a devout Catholic family and educated in parochial schools, George would, at times, disrupt the flow of life with challenging religious questions. As he grew older, his thinking became more spiritual and less in keeping with organized religion. His ways were gentle. Qualities of the human spirit—love and compassion, forgiveness, a sense of responsibility, harmony, and contentment—were important to him. Rules, regulations and dogma were not. He felt such things were man-made, limiting and exclusionary, as if you were being asked to join a private club. His mother attributed this religious journey to his six years in the military. But, actually, his search for understanding was simply George being George.

He loved taking tests, and his thirst for information led him to take, and to pass, numerous exams. George, therefore, held a variety of licenses. He had:

√ an Economics Degree
√ a Real Estate License
√ a Travel Agent card
√ a Stationary Engineer's License
√ a Supervising Electrician's License, and
√ an Electrical Contractor's License.

And he was:

√ a journeyman electrician for IBEW Local #134
√ a past President of Toastmasters, and
√ certified in many phases of carpet cleaning by the IICRC.

As a child, George had a difficult time fitting into the educational mold of conventional schooling. His self-image suffered, because his true brain power was not recognized in the school setting of his youth. As an adult, however, he was able to pursue interests and directions of his own choosing. His choices took him down a variety of roads and he flourished.

Good for you, George. You realized that your potential was unlimited. Genuine self-effacing modesty, however, prevented him from understanding that he was truly an intellectual powerhouse.

George never talked about people. Instead, he was a fount of ideas. Someone commented, "Most people talk about the weather or the Cubs. George would come in and say, 'I have an idea I think you'd like.' Then he would tell you something that you never, ever would have thought about on your own."

Never boring. Sometimes confusing. Always intriguing.

Shortly after George died, my cousin's husband, Lee, sent me a note:

> *Dear Betty,*
>
> *Hi.*
>
> *We would like to see you again as soon as possible.*
>
> *It would just be nice to see you and do things together.*
>
> *Remember, George liked us, and you guys were one of the weirdest couples we know.*
>
> *So, let's get together and do something George liked, such as talking about whether cats float in the Black Sea.*
>
> *Love, Lee*

How many times did I hear him say: "existentialism is a humanism." The number of times he told me that one equals the number of times I asked him to please explain to me its meaning "once again." Even now, I can't remember exactly what it means. I'll have to check the dictionary and then I probably still won't understand. *I'm so sorry, George. I wasn't the deep thinker in our twosome.*

Another favorite saying of his was: "FEAR is False Evidence Appearing Real."

And then there was: "Choose to live from abundance, not from scarcity."

I always appreciated his measured, thoughtful response when I would come up with impulsive thoughts and actions.

"Go ahead and do that if you must, Betty," he'd say. "I'll help you out of the mess that you're going to create."

What a guy. *I'm so sorry, George. I created some awesome messy situations, and you never failed to come to my rescue. How did you put up with me?*

Gardening was one of George's favorite pastimes. I believe he felt a spiritual connection to the earth and its bounty. He created something called "gardening in the grass." One year, he planted forty tomato plants in the lawn. That way, he never had to weed around them. He simply cut the grass up and down the rows of plants.

Forty plants. He didn't even eat tomatoes.

Do you realize the bumper crop we had that year? We had tomato juice, tomato soup, bacon, lettuce and tomato sandwiches, stewed tomatoes, sliced tomatoes and hives from eating so many tomatoes.

We couldn't give them away fast enough. I loved it, because I loved him.

Spiritual connections didn't just come through gardening. George lived a connected life. Every night when he went to bed and every morning before he arose, he would raise his right arm straight up. Sometimes, he would raise both arms, but mostly it was his right arm.

"What are you doing, George?" I would ask.

"I'm connecting to The Source," he would say.

It was an amazing sight, to see this 6'2" gentle giant plugging in to "The Source" of spiritual energy with his big ole, gorgeous Popeye arms.

He felt that everything came from "The Source" and that somehow "The Source" had to do with the sun. I never asked him, but do you think that maybe, in some way, he felt that the sun and The Son were connected in meaning?

He had a direct connection. We all do. Unfortunately, not everyone senses theirs.

But, fortunately, George sensed his. Not only did he sense it, but he was able to tap into it, as well. That connection made a difference in his life back then. And it is making an even bigger difference today.

The "I'm connecting to The Source" was clue #1 that George was in a transitional state and growing in enlightenment. I didn't get the message because I had no idea that there was any such thing as a sign, much less knew how to read one. Shortly, however, my ability to read signs would change in dramatic fashion.

4 CHANGING RESIDENCES—AND A SIGN

We had lived in our house, on New Hampshire Avenue, for 30 years. It was a lovely 100-year-old home with beautiful wood interiors, stained glass windows, a huge dining room, a grand front porch with a swing, and a finished third floor. The home was on half an acre, quite a large piece of property by city standards. It was a happy house and the site of enjoyable parties and quiet times.

When we first moved in, George decided to refinish the oak front hall staircase. Each stair had a dust corner, a triangular shaped piece of tin that fit into the corner of every step so that dust would not accumulate. The rounded corners made cleaning quite easy.

The stairs and dust corners were all heavily painted. When beginning the refinishing job, George pried off the corners. Curious to see what they looked like underneath the layers of paint, he took them down into the basement to clean them.

When he removed the paint from one of the pieces, he was surprised at what he discovered. Coming upstairs with the newly cleaned and polished piece, he said, "Check this out, Betty!" Underneath the coats of paint was a beautiful monogram of intricate design. Each piece contained the interwoven initials: G.P.

"Oh George," I said, "you were meant to live in this house!" We looked at each other silently, not fully knowing what we were experiencing. I still didn't have a clue about signs and we had just received a huge one.

Time evaporates and after years of cutting the grass, shoveling the snow and doing the general upkeep of happy homeowning, we began to view our beautiful home and huge piece of corner property as more of a chore and less of a joy. Both girls were finished with college, and George and I were looking forward to some lifestyle changes.

Since our land was already divided into two lots of record, we decided to build a home on our "backyard," then sell our existing home and move into the brand-new abode. After clearing up a few glitches with City Hall and a cranky neighbor, we were on our way.

Our architect lived around the corner, our general contractor lived down the street and our electrical contractor lived in our house. With George doing the electrical plans and work himself, and with tremendous assistance from his brother, Joe, the entire project soon became both a family and a neighborhood affair. How perfect to watch the birth of our new home from an up-close-and-personal vantage point.

For the most part, George enjoyed the project. At times, he would throw a typical George tantrum when something electrical didn't go quite right. Muttering, then yelling, then throwing things, then instantly calming down, he would get back to work, all the while seeming oblivious to our yelling back and laughing at him. He always just needed to get it out of his system so he could resolve whatever problem had caused the eruption.

Work began in April, 2001, and that very October we moved into our gorgeous finished, brand-new home, complete with the monogrammed "G P" dust corners that we had moved from their original location. Let the fun begin and the good times roll.

Although we had moved in, there were still numerous things that needed to be completed. Some were major: sanding, priming and painting all the wood trim in the house, and staining all of the doors. Some were minor: just simple finishing touches here and there.

There wasn't any need to hurry. We were taking our time choosing colors and making choices. Did we want high gloss, semigloss or muted? Should we stain, or paint, the mullion bars? We had all the time in the world, and we were working on it together, thoroughly enjoying the work and each other.

It was the middle of December, 2001, and we had lived in our new home for two months. Margaret was in the living room, fixing Christmas decorations. I was in the kitchen, making cookies.

Somewhere in the house, something crashed and broke.

"Moll, are you OK?"

"Yes."

"What was that?"

"I don't know."

Together we walked from room to room trying to solve the mystery. Above the windows in the dining room were hanging blue and white, dated, Scandinavian decorative plates. For no apparent reason, one of the plates had fallen off the wall. Its hook was still there in the wall, but the plate was smashed on the floor. I saw that the date on the plate was 1969. How odd—1969 had been the year of our marriage.

I was still in the dining room, picking up pieces of broken china, when George came home from work. Pointing to the empty space on the wall, I said, "What's up with the plate, George? Are you planning on leaving me?"

"I'd never leave you, Betty," he said.

I was kidding him when I had said it. I was teasing him about "leaving me for a blonde."

I never dreamed that in a month he would be leaving forever.

The fallen plate, dated with the year of our marriage, was a huge message. Not knowing it was a heads-up sign, I completely missed the meaning. If I had understood, what could or would I have done differently?

Nothing. I was powerless to stop the events of the coming month.

In retrospect, I believe that George knew he was leaving, but didn't understand the timetable. Maybe he did; I certainly did not. I had no clue that there even was a timetable, let alone one so imminent.

GEORGE'S FINAL FOUR DAYS

2002:

Friday, January 18:

We attended a retirement party for my school principal. It was a delightful time with my friends and colleagues. Everyone knew George because when he wasn't on a job, he always came to school to help me carry things to the room, to bring me lunch or to help me get the room ready for the afternoon kindergarten class. He was definitely part of my classroom management system. I remember dancing with him that evening, thinking how great he looked and how happy we were.

Saturday, January 19:

I was a bit stressed from work and "the house." Looking back, I think I was doing a lot of "blah, blah, blah" and "waaa, waaa, waaa"; crabby stuff about this and that. I remember complaining about a stick on the garage roof. A stupid stick; who cared? My last conscious memory of George at home is seeing him on a ladder, getting that damn stick down. It is etched in my mind. That stupid, damn stick. Just to please me.

Sunday, January 20:

It was about 11:15 in the morning, and I can still picture the scene as if it happened a moment ago. We were upstairs. George was standing in the bedroom and I was standing at the bathroom doorway. I have no idea what prompted me to ask the question, but I turned to him, took his arms, looked directly into his eyes and said: "Is there something you need to tell me,

George? If there is, I want to know. It's not just about you. It's about us and I need to know. I love you."

He replied: "No, there's nothing." And, with that, I actually saw clouds pass through his eyes from right to left. As long as I live, I will never forget that sight: as if a door had opened briefly and closed just as quickly. A glimpse into the unknown. It was an incredible exchange: brief, but powerful and loving. Thank God it was loving, for it was something I would later replay over and over and over in my mind.

Monday, January 21:

George worked around the house, shopped at the grocery store, made a tuna casserole for dinner, played Trivial Pursuit with Molly and her friend, Ellen (he won), and picked up Kate at the airport.

I spent the day at the funeral of a family friend. I returned home in time to eat his delicious dinner. He, I remember thinking later, didn't eat anything. I will never, ever be able to eat that dish again.

It was 6:00 PM. George was going to take Kate back to her

apartment. I decided, at the last moment, to go, too. There were four of us in the car: George, Kate, myself, and a neighbor who came along for the ride.

Arriving in Lincoln Park, George carried Kate's suitcase up to her third-floor walk-up apartment. Previously, each time when he had walked up those stairs he would be out of breath. This time, after carrying her suitcase up the three flights, he commented to Kate: "Hey, pal, I did it this time and I'm not out of breath at all."

Checking the bathroom for bogeymen in her studio apartment, he turned to her before leaving and said, "I love you, pal."

She replied, "I love you, too. Bye, Dad."

He returned to the car, getting into the driver's seat, and we headed home. It was 7:00 PM. There were three of us in the car: George, myself and the neighbor. Of this you will hear more. But the short version is—

Talking and laughing, we drove less than a mile.

... And, suddenly, George was dead ...

... After leaving the hospital, the neighbor and I drove home. Now there were just two of us in the smashed car; myself and the neighbor. There was no laughing, no talking. There was total silence. Total dead silence. It was 10:00 PM.

Dead.

Impossible.

Surreal.

Within four short hours, my life had drastically and completely changed—from attending a funeral during the day to having to begin planning one that night ...

... Dear, Dear George ...

How will I ever survive?

Surreal.

Impossible.

Dead.

PART TWO: THE END

THE CRISIS—IN SLOW MOTION ...

Let me backtrack.
On the way home from Kate's, the seating arrangement in the car, again, was as follows: George was driving, the neighbor was in the passenger seat, and I was in the back seat directly behind the neighbor. From my vantage point, I was able to view the entire scene.

I remember making a comment about the store we were passing; that perhaps it would be a good place to look for the futon or sleeper sofa that we were interested in purchasing. When I turned my head forward, I noticed that the traffic light had changed to red, but George wasn't stopping. Several things started happening at once.

Just as I was saying, "George, what are you doing?" I saw him lift his head, as if looking up at someone, turn it slightly to the left, and say in a very soft, very gentle voice, "Oh, help me, please help ..."

With that, the neighbor said, "George, you've got to stop!" and, turning left to look at him, put his arm out to brace George as he began to slump over the steering wheel.

We smashed into the car in front of us.

(Ironically, it was the type of car that George had, just that day, talked about purchasing. We were in a Saturn and the other vehicle was an Isuzu Rodeo.)

With the car stopped, I jumped out, ran to the other side, and opened George's door. At that point, I saw that he was still breathing. Rubbing my hand on his chest, I said, "I love you, I love you, I love you and I'm going to get you help."

My mind was thinking, "How the hell am I going to help him? I can't get his body out of the car and, if I could, he'd have to lie down on the street!"

I then ran to the car we had just hit and said *I was so sorry, but I thought my husband had suffered a heart attack* and asked *if they were all right.*

They assured me they were fine and that we needed to help George. Running back to George, I began trying to direct traffic around us. Everything was happening at once. The stunned neighbor sat in the car with George.

The accident occurred in Chicago, at the intersection of Halsted and Diversey. A firehouse happened to be located right around the corner. I looked up to see a firefighter, on foot, dodging through traffic to reach us. Immediately assessing the scene, he spoke into his radio, "Chief, we need an ambulance."

My brain thought, "Dear Lord, please send someone I know."

I have no idea how or why that came into my mind. We live, and I work, in an area of the city where there are numerous police and firefighter families. I must have thought that the odds were pretty good that someone I knew would be on duty. Still, it was a strange prayer, uttered in desperation and need.

The people on the street were marvelous. A girl gave me her cell phone to use and I called Molly at home. I'm surprised I even remembered our number. I told Molly that we had been involved in an accident, and that they were going to send an ambulance to take Dad to the hospital, but that I was certain everything would be OK and that she didn't need to come. Could she just call and let Kate know?

That accomplished, I turned to see ambulance #43 pull up. "Oh, dear God!" I said when I saw that the first paramedic out was a woman I knew. "Thank you for coming to help us!" My spontaneous prayer had been answered.

It took several firemen to get George out of the car.

One of them was a man whom George had worked with at McCormick Place Convention Center.

So now, *two* of the people who were helping George knew us. Not that they did anything differently for us than they would have for any other person in need ... but, it was just such a comfort to me to hear them call him by name, knowing that they were doing everything possible to help us in this impossible situation.

And, as if this weren't enough, it turned out that I knew three of the responding police officers, as well. They were handling everything ...

... and filling out the paperwork about the accident ...

... and sending George's body to the coroner's with minimal distress for me. They took care of George as if he were one of their own. Now there were *five people* who knew us who were helping George.

Several years prior to all this, George had saved my life by giving me mouth-to-mouth resuscitation and chest compressions. Later, when I was recovering, I had asked him "How did you know how to do that?"

He said, "You dragged me to that CPR class; that's how I knew."

But standing in the middle of that street, I could not return the favor.

I stood by helplessly.

It was now dark out and I could see the lights that were on inside the ambulance, illuminating the work being done on George. It was something I couldn't bear to watch.

I stepped to one side to remove it from my line of vision. The *Streetwise* newspaper man came, put his arm around my shoulders, and held me up as we watched. He was about 6'7" tall and his kindness was just as huge. I will never forget his gentle strength.

Our neighbor had moved the car to the curb, and, as he walked back toward us, I said, "He's dead. Can you believe it? He's dead."

"No, he's not; he can't be," the neighbor replied.

"Yes, he is. I know it!"

With that simple exchange, we just stood there.

Numb.

Waiting to be told what we should do next.

The Chief came over and said that they were going to take George to the hospital, and that I should ride up front in his car, and that the neighbor should follow in our car, our smashed car.

It was then that I truly realized that things were not going well with George. If he had been stabilized, I would have been riding in the ambulance with him. Riding with the Chief was not a good sign.

When I was 24, my sister, my only sibling, had died a very sudden, tragic and violent death. At that time, I learned, in an instant, what was important in this life and what was not. I was—abruptly—to relearn that lesson.

AT THE HOSPITAL

Arriving at the hospital, I immediately went to the registration desk of the emergency room.

As we were beginning the necessary paperwork, someone came to get me and I found myself being taken into a private waiting room. I call it the grief room. Another sign that things weren't going well.

My neighbor and I sat there in silence for a brief time. The door opened and a nurse asked me to go with her to the ER area where they were attending to George.

Because George was still receiving CPR, the monitor gave the appearance that his heart was still beating. I stood at his feet, staring in disbelief, trying to comprehend the incomprehensible.

One of the doctors came over to me and said, "We have been doing this for 20 minutes."

"It isn't working, is it?" I replied.

He responded, "We will do it for as long as you want us to."

I heard myself say, "Thank you for your incredible effort, but I think you can stop."

All activity ceased.

The silence was deafening.

Somehow, I needed to connect with George. As I stood at the end of the table he was lying on, I took hold of his feet and spoke directly to him:

"Do you know what a wonderful father you've been? Do you know what a wonderful husband you have been? Thank you, Georgie. I love you. I love you... "

... ...

... There was nothing left to do. I kissed his feet and then turned around, to see the paramedic that I knew, dissolved in tears.

"How do you do this job?" I asked.

She replied, "It's not easy, especially when you know the people involved. I am so sorry."

I was helped back to the grief room.

Upon opening the door, I saw that Kate and Moll were both there. I'm not certain why they decided to come, but Margaret must have sensed an urgency in my voice when I called her from the street. I was relieved to see them.

And, I was most grateful to their friends for bringing them to the hospital. We were all together at a time when we would most need to be with one another.

Kate asked, "How is he doing?"

In a voice that matched his flat-line heartbeat, I replied, "He's fucking dead."

Never having been known to use raw language, I thus began my up-close-and-personal relationship with the word "fuck." For the next three months running, I used it as a noun, a verb, an adjective, an adverb, a dangling participle; you name it. I used it on its own or coupled with a string of words.

I told my 87-year-old mother that, if that was the worst thing I did to get through this, then I wasn't doing too badly; she would just have to deal with it. She understood.

My daughters and friends understood, as well.

But George, who in our 33 years of marriage always let me do whatever I wanted to do, wouldn't have understood. He would have told me to "Stop it, Betty!"

The next moments in that little room were filled with the complete spectrum of emotions.

Silence.
Wailing.
Yelling.
Nausea.
Crying.
Disbelief.

You name it. It took place. There was a surge of emotion that would not be contained.

A grief counselor who, I'm sure, in her line of work has seen it all, opened the door. She asked if I would like to see George.

I was taken to a private room where George's body was lying.

With all the tubes and apparatus removed, he looked as if he were sleeping. Shutting the door, the counselor left the two of us alone.

I sat down beside him and tried to comprehend the magnitude and meaning of what was taking place. Linking my arm through his, and putting my legs beside his body up on the gurney, I talked to him:

"Send me some vibes, George. Help me figure out what I'm supposed to do."

That's about all I said. Mostly, I just looked at his beautifully kind face and his strong arms.

It was a private time, filled with private touches. How grateful I am that I had that moment alone with him.

I have no idea the length of time that passed, but the hospital personnel were generous and respectful of my (our) privacy.

A knock at the door.

I said, "Come in." The door opened. It was the grief counselor, and behind her I could see my two daughters. My two devastated daughters.

I didn't move. I couldn't. She asked if I was OK, and I replied, "He had the most beautiful penis."

She nodded gently and Kate said, "Mom ... "

"It's OK," I said to Kate. "That's where you came from, and it's beautiful."

If he were alive, I never would have said something of that nature. If he were alive he would have sat up and said, "Betty, with everything you could have said, did you have to say *that*? You're embarrassing me!"

It took a few weeks before Kate asked me if I knew what I had said in the hospital. Yes, I knew exactly what I had said. They were words spoken from my heart ... words that mirrored the realization that a beautiful and meaningful part of my life had ended.

Three brokenhearted women were then left alone with the body of the man who had loved them, cared for them, tolerated them and adored them. The feelings were mutual. The three of us sat and looked at this silent person who had rarely been silent or still his entire lifetime.

Margaret spoke first: "Where did he go?"

"Well, Moll," I said, "I have no idea, but all his life he said that we are made up of incredible energy and that energy cannot be destroyed. It just goes into something else. So, he's here. We just can't see him."

I'm not certain of our exact conversation in that room, but we each talked to him, talked to one another, and said our "good-byes."

I removed the wedding ring from his finger and put it on mine. Then I crawled on top of his body to give him one last hug, knowing that he would not hug back.

Not being a medical person, I didn't realize that my body compressing his would bring forth a gurgling sound. For an instant, the sound let me think the unthinkable: *It's all a mistake. He's still alive!*

That brief instant over, I returned to reality.

A protective fog, called shock, was beginning to cover me. It enveloped me for a year and a half.

I don't remember leaving George, but we somehow returned to the grief room to collect our belongings, his belongings, and our supportive friends.

Standing outside the hospital, we decided that we would drive to my mother's, so that we could explain to her what had just transpired.

Explain? How could we explain the unexplainable, the inexplicable?

On their way home, Kate and Moll called my mother and their Uncle Joe, one of George's brothers, and then their Aunt Mary, one of George's sisters. How they were able to do it, I'll never know. I called no one. The only person I wanted to call wasn't able to answer the phone. Besides, I didn't know his new number.

We had almost reached my mother's when the neighbor decided he wanted to go home. I dropped him off and I continued on alone, driving the smashed car, sitting where George belonged.

Gathering at my mother's, we all began our grieving. Bound by our love for George, we were present together.

Talking, then silent.
Silent, then talking.
Trying to get our brains to compute and accept the unacceptable.

I felt as if someone had smashed me in the face with a two-by-four and had cut off both my arms. My body and brain were totally incapacitated.

But three thoughts of consolation kept going through my mind:

1) *I'm so glad I had been with him.*

2) I had asked the heavens to send a responding paramedic that I would know. *All total, there were five people who knew us who came to help.* One paramedic, one firefighter and three police officers. I had asked for one, and five were sent. In the midst of it all, at an unfamiliar intersection in a huge city, five people with a connection to us were part of the response team. I was beginning to realize that awesome help surrounded me ... awesome help both seen and unseen ... awesome help both known and unknown ...

   And I also thought

3) *Thank you*—to whomever has been sending the help.

BACK AT HOME

George loved to cook. In recent years, he had done most, if not all, of the cooking at home. I am able to cook but, honestly, do not enjoy doing so.

Reaching home, we entered the house through the door nearest the kitchen. Inside, looking at our beautiful, new kitchen, I asked Moll how she liked her cornflakes served. The effort required to make that dish was going to equal the amount of effort I was henceforth going to be able to put forth into preparing meals.

I didn't realize it at that moment, but the kitchen and the dining room, where we had last eaten together, were going to be the most difficult areas of the home for me to keep revisiting.

Especially, meals in the dining room. Impossible ...

A wave of sadness came over me; the first of innumerable waves, as I realized that I would never again have Rock Cornish hen on a bed of wild rice, with fresh asparagus, served to me with George's style and flair.

So the three of us walked into the kitchen and sat down. It was 12:15 AM. There were no tears. The tears were certainly there; they were just so deep within that it would take a while for them to reach the surface.

I went to the room where I keep my school things and got out a sheet of poster board and a big, fat black marker. I wrote:

```
Our Georgie is dead
and our hearts are
broken.
```

I hung the sign in a front window for everyone to see. One of the girls asked, "What are you doing?"

"I'm putting up a sign so everyone will know. I don't have the energy to call people. Maybe someone will see the sign and spread the word. Sort of like smoke signals. I hope the information will be passed around."

We live in an area (Norwood Park) that is small-town-like in nature, even though it is part of the great city of Chicago. My parents moved there when I was in college. Having lived there myself for many years both before and after marriage, even though I didn't know everyone, I knew very many of our neighbors. I now wanted them to share in our grief.

Early in the morning, a man walking his dog saw the sign, went home and said to his wife, "I hope Georgie is their dog."

"No," she replied, "it's her husband."

The sign worked better than I could have imagined. Word spread like wildfire. Our dear neighbors did, indeed, share in our grief.

Meanwhile, the three of us kept sitting there. All of our important, individual agendas had become insignificant ... unimportant ... useless ... thrown out the window ...

Now what were we supposed to do? I'd never previously had my husband drop dead right before my eyes. There was no script for us to follow.

It dawned on me, in slow motion, that I wouldn't be going to school for several days. My first thought was that I needed to get that base covered.

I have come to realize that Jeanine, the daughter of my neighbor, Sue, and the woman who was working with me in my kindergarten classroom at that time, is part of my life plan. I wonder how we may have been connected in other lifetimes. Not only was our working relationship one of perfect harmony but she knew, and enjoyed knowing, George, as well.

At this time, Jeanine was going to night school to get her master's degree. Since George had also gone to school at night, he understood her pain. "Play the game, Jeanine," he would tell her.

In Jeanine's words "that was the best advice he had ever given me." George and Jeanine had grown to be true friends.

I couldn't call her. How could I tell her this horrendous news? She needed to know by morning, but my calling her was not an option.

So I picked up the phone to call my friend and neighbor, Sue. It was one of the few numbers I was able to dial in the coming days.

Poor Sue. Every time someone in my family dies, she gets a call. Plus, as I've said, Sue happens to be Jeanine's mother. She would tell Jeanine. One problem was solved.

It was now a little after 12:30 AM and one of Sue's sons answered the phone.

"This is Betty Portenlanger," I said. "May I please speak with your mother? I know it is terribly late, but I need to speak with her. It's very important."

Sue came to the phone. Because of the lateness of the hour, I knew that it would take a moment for my words to register: "Sue, this is Betty. George is dead." Would she please call and tell Jeanine? I simply couldn't. "Also, please tell Jeanine that I will be sending class work for each day." Questions and explanations followed, as we briefly spoke.

I made one more call to a colleague, Donna. I wanted her to know the news, for work purposes. I also wanted her to know because we were friends. Our families had vacationed together, and she had grown to know, and enjoy, and love George.

I called, our conversation was brief, and ended with her being left stunned by the news.

The doorbell rang. There stood Sue. Kate, Moll, Sue and I then sat together, trying to get our brains to accept the events of the evening.

It was taking a while for things to sink in.
That's it?
It's over? Can't be.
It is.
Disbelief made us reject the reality.

12:45 AM. The phone rang. It was the organ donor lady.

"My, you work late," I said.

In an exchange that cannot be described in writing, we discussed donating various parts of George. I was informed that, because his body had been shut down when his heart had exploded, the large organs were not usable. However, there were other ways in which he could be of help.

My daughters looked at me, aghast, as I asked for their permission at each new body part request.

I was giving away pieces of their father. He didn't need them any more; perhaps he could be of benefit to others.

They listened, at length, to one side of the conversation.

Finally, my answer to one last question revealed that George had had hepatitis. I couldn't remember which type. (It didn't end up mattering. The fact that he'd had any hepatitis made all of his parts unacceptable.)

A or B? I knew it wasn't C. "I think it was B. Help me, Moll; you're the one in Sports Medicine. Which one was it?"

It got a bit bizarre with letters flying all around. Finally, Sue put a stop to it. "It was hepatitis F. U.! Now, hang up the phone." I thanked the woman for calling and put down the receiver.

Comic relief set in. It was like a scene from "Saturday Night Live" or from some Monty Python sketch.

George had a dislike and distrust of large institutions. His health issues as a child had caused him not to be particularly fond of the medical profession.

I now know why he needed to endure the tremendous suffering from hepatitis. It was so that he would be able to reclaim his own body at the time of his death.

Here I was, trying to give him away to an institution that made him uncomfortable. But he was able to snatch himself back at the last moment.

We were all exhausted. Sue went home. The three of us went to bed. Before I did, I lit a candle; the first of many that I would light throughout the days ahead. I also left the desk lamp on so it wouldn't be dark for him—just in case he came home.

# PART THREE: HONORING THE DEPARTED

THE 'GRADUATION TO HEAVEN' PARTY

A flurry of activity filled the next two days. The planning of how we would say good-bye to our George consumed us.

Early the next morning I did call Jeanine, after all, although I have no recollection of dialing the phone or of the conversation that took place. She, however, will never forget hearing me say "This is Betty Portenlanger. George Portenlanger died last night." How odd that I would say it in that way; that formal, detached way. Perhaps I was trying to separate myself from the situation.

But poor Jeanine; she went to school, walked into the classroom, and saw that the clock had stopped: it had stopped at 7:00 PM, the exact time of George's death. What were the chances of that happening?

In her grief, she gathered some faculty members together to tell them the sad news. Miraculously, she then carried on with class. I know she did it as a gift to me, and as a tribute to George; still, I don't know how she was able to pull it off.

During our walks around the park, George and I used to talk about anything and everything.

Sometimes we would walk in silence, enjoying "just being;" being alive and being together. When we did talk, the subjects were interesting and varied, just like George.

On more than one occasion, George had said that, when he died, he wanted to be thrown into a volcano.

"Give me a break, George! How am I supposed to get your big, old body up to the volcano and throw you in?"

"No, Betty. You have me cremated. Then it will be easy."

I'd never thought about cremation and I had *certainly* never thought about volcanoes.

"You'd better write that down, George. I love your family, and they will think I've totally 'lost it' if I claim you said that one."

So he did write it down, though never did I dream I'd have to carry out his wish.

Before we could do that, however, we would have to honor George in Chicago, somehow.

At this time in his life, George had certain "count me out" views, regarding organized religion. We decided therefore, to have a celebration of his life in our home; the home that he had built and had lived in for only three months.

It would be a type of "Open House," but not the usual type of Open House most people hold.

We called it the "George's Graduation To Heaven" party. The hours were to be from 1:00 PM to 9:00 PM. We made our preparations, and waited for the people to arrive.

At ten minutes to one, Kate, Moll, my mother and I sat in our living room.

"What if we give this party and nobody comes?" I said. Looking out the window, I didn't see a soul in sight. How awful! Maybe this was a bad idea.

One o'clock arrived—and so did the people. During the next eight hours, over 650 people arrived, to be exact. I didn't know that we knew that many people! It was amazing. At times, they were lined up down the street, waiting to get in.

Not only did people arrive, but food arrived, as well. I hadn't really planned anything. I hadn't even thought about that aspect. But dear family, neighbors and friends had thought of it and they were amazing. To this day, I am overwhelmed when I think of the generosity, the true kindness, and the love that poured forth.

It was beautifully unbelievable. The cakes, the salads, the sandwiches, the beverages, the everything. Nothing was left out. Plates, cups, napkins, silverware, coffee. I know that everyone who contributed to the success of that occasion will forgive me if I single out my neighbor, Bernie. Her enormous and superbly delicious pasta salad was out of this world.

George had dearly loved my sister's children, Beth and Dan, and their spouses, Steve and Amy. They held a special place in his heart, for many reasons. Now, coming together in sadness, they were tireless in their efforts that day—in both their emotional and physical efforts. No wonder he loved them. No wonder I do, too.

Moments big and small made the event memorable. Sheila appeared with her rescue kit, which contained, among other things, Kleenex and chapstick. George's sister, Rita, and her family offered invaluable emotional support. Hai and Ingrid worked quietly and unobtrusively. Women from my church arrived and organized crowd control and the signing of the guest book. It was as if everyone had previously worked together as a team, numerous times. What a scene! What a joyous celebration for our dear George. He was the only one missing.

Periodically, throughout the day and evening, we would give a cheer for George and the beautiful house he had built. We would praise, in particular, his electrical work. Someone would flicker the lights and a rousing cheer would go up for George and his expertise. Broken-hearted as we all were, we celebrated.

Because I had incorporated George into my kindergarten activities, the children and their families all knew him. What a support system they provided, as they came to share in our grief. Their presence and their kind words will last in my heart for a lifetime.

Mary Lou, a grandmother of one of my former students, wrote:

Dear Betty,

When my granddaughter, Emily, was about 3 years old, I had her in the stroller and we were walking down Devon Avenue.

A very long funeral procession was passing and I pointed out the funeral flags on the cars, and was explaining this funeral process to her, when I felt a strong pressure (like a hand) on my shoulder. It seemed to turn my body full forward toward the street...

An awareness flooded my entire being ...

I strongly felt a need to express gratitude for all the

good and beauty this person-unknown-to-me brought to our world ...

And, ever since then, each morning I think about those who will finish their journey on earth on that day and I thank them sincerely for the good and beauty they have brought to our world ...

A deep sense of gratitude fills me now just as it did that day on Devon Avenue when the funeral procession drove by.

I tell you all of this so that you will know where it came from, when I share with you my gratitude to George, and for his gift to all of us.

For you, I send a bit of John O'Donohue:

Matins

Somewhere, out at the edges, the night
Is turning and the waves of darkness
Begin to brighten the shore of dawn.

The heavy dark falls back to earth
And the freed air goes wild with light,
The heart fills with fresh, bright breath
And thoughts stir to give birth to colour.

I arise today

In the name of Silence
Womb of the Word,
In the name of Stillness
Home of Belonging,
In the name of the Solitude
Of the Soul and the Earth.

I arise today

Blessed by all things,
Wings of breath,
Delight of eyes,
Wonder of whisper,
Intimacy of touch,
Eternity of soul,
Urgency of thought,
Miracle of health,
Embrace of God.

May I live this day

Compassionate of heart,
Gentle in word,
Gracious in awareness,
Courageous in thought,
Generous in love.

Much Love to you and yours,

Mary Lou

It is because of this letter that now, whenever I see an ambulance, I offer a prayer for the person in need, for those that love him or her, and for those who are giving them medical assistance. And, whenever I see a funeral procession, I offer a prayer of thanks for the life that has ended, and offer a blessing to send them on their way.

Cindy, a mother of two of my former students, wrote, in a beautiful note, "I am reminded of a line from *Steel Magnolias*, 'I'd rather have three minutes of wonderful than a lifetime of nothing special'."

I had been given such a treasure and I knew it. I had been given a lifetime of wonderful.

Another mom, Julie, wrote:

> *My favorite George story is about when my Steven was in kindergarten, and every time he would see George, he would go up to him, and say, "Hi, Mr. Portenlanger. Do you remember me? I'm Steven."*
>
> *And George would always say, "Of course I remember you, Steven."*
>
> *That ritual was repeated countless times, and George never failed to respond with patience and politeness to Steven's introduction. It was a beautiful interaction between the two and a delight to observe.*

It was especially heartwarming to receive the handcrafted drawings and cards from the children:

"Even though you live alone now, I hope you will be OK."

"I'm sorry the Mr. Portenlanger diyd. I hope your vacashins are alrit without him. It's alrit to cry, it let's the sad out of you."

Especially poignant was the "I'm Sorry" balloon that bobbed around our house for weeks. As it deflated and slowly sunk to the floor it was symbolic of our emotional state.

This delightful picture was created by one of my students, named Jessica. It shows a smiling, golden-winged George soaring among the rainbows.

The 'Graduation to Heaven' Party

I also loved Margaret's handwritten note on the fireplace mantel:

Papa,

You were THE BEST!

I will miss you & I LOVE YOU!

♥ Molly

During the party, I stood in the same spot for eight and a half hours and, at the end of the evening, I could hardly walk.
   That didn't matter. What mattered was that we had done it. We had done it for George. As one child commented to her grandmother: "This was the best party I've ever been to." I know that George was there, and I know that he appreciated each and every kindness shown. We were truly blessed.

There were three other private ceremonies held in remembrance of George:

The evening after the gathering in our home, a private viewing was held for immediate family members. George's brother Stephen, a deacon in the Catholic Church, created a beautiful service for this memorial. It was a way for his siblings to say goodbye to their dear brother.

As a member of the United Methodist Church, I felt I needed to have some type of religious conclusion to George's earthly life, held in my church. George certainly didn't need it. I needed it.

So, after about two weeks, Kate, Moll and I took George's ashes to the chapel at my church. The three of us, along with my minister, held a brief, but meaningful "ceremony."

During this time, I made a presentation to each of the girls of three gifts that I felt represented their father:

- ♥ First, the book, *As A Man Thinketh*, by James Allen. George loved this book and I think he actually memorized it.
- ♥ Second, three cards with positive affirmations that he used to read every day.
- ♥ Third, a sand dollar, to remind them of the wonderful trips we had taken together as a family; especially the numerous trips involving oceans.

Returning home after this last observance, I felt we had covered all the bases.

Well, almost all of the bases. We had taken care of family, friends and the three of us ...

But it remained that we take care of George and honor his volcano wish. How in the world was I going to accomplish that?

As my friend, Maureen, has taught me to say: "All will be revealed in the fullness of time." There was no need for concern on my part. I simply had to stand back and watch life unfold.

GRIEF = FEAR

In his book, *A Grief Observed*, C. S. Lewis opens with the line, "No one ever told me that grief felt so much like fear." I hadn't known that, either. I now knew.

As the days went by, I became filled with thoughts of "How am I going to do this? How am I going to do this emotionally, physically, spiritually and financially? I don't think that I am going to make it."

It was a real fear, an overwhelming fear that I was not going to survive. I knew what George had said about F-E-A-R, but I didn't care. He wasn't the one standing here trying to figure things out. I was here and I was afraid. I was overwhelmingly afraid. It was like nothing I had ever before experienced.

In the past, when there had been difficulty or sadness, I relied on my support system; my support system named George. He had taken care of me for 33 years.

I still needed that care. I still wanted that care. There was a strong sense that he was still around, but I couldn't see him, hear him or touch him. I could just feel his presence, a treasured presence with which I would have to learn how to live.

During these last 33 years, I had always talked to my God and to my George. I never could physically see God, but I still talked with Him. And now, I couldn't physically see George, either, but I still talked with him. I totally believed in the existence of both and I received incredible help from both, as well. Even though I could no longer see George, I would still talk to him whenever and wherever I needed to. My mantra became: "I love you, I miss you, I thank you."

So that I could keep things organized, I started a folder marked "George's Exit Plan." In it, I put all of the information I could find regarding his death. And when I needed to make a decision about something, I would put his Irish cap on my head to help me think. He was so smart and so wise that I thought his wisdom would transfer into me if I wore his cap. I trusted this to work, and it did.

"I love you, I miss you, I thank you."

Kate, Moll and I all struggled to regain our balance. Our grief came in George's size: XL. If we hadn't known the joy before, we wouldn't have known this sorrow now. The height of our blessings equaled the depths of our despair. His ultimate internal spontaneous-combustion was not going to be easy to absorb.

One night, shortly after George's death, Kate sat at the dinner table with her hand up, as George had always done when connecting to "The Source."

"Put your hand down," I said. " 'The Source' came and got one person I love. I don't need another one to leave."

I thought about the plate's falling off the wall, the clouds I had seen in George's eyes and of his connecting to "The Source"; all were pieces to a puzzle.

I didn't understand the puzzle, but I was beginning to connect the dots. When clouds cover the sun, it is still there. You just can't see it, but it still shines brightly. So, too, with George: I couldn't see him, but I knew that he was still here, shining as brightly as ever.

What we had as a loving family cost nothing, but it was priceless. Kate was right on target when she commented, "We had no unresolved issues." How fortunate to be able to say that and how comforting. As difficult as our loss was, unresolved issues would have made it an insurmountable catastrophe.

I made the girls promise that they wouldn't change their lives for me. They must continue on. I would survive.

I came home one day to hear Margaret say into the phone, "He could do everything. Now we'll have to ask ten people to do all the things he used to do all by himself."

When she hung up the phone, I said, "He'll still help us. And he will help in ways we can't even imagine. Just ask him. Or, write him a note. Just make sure that you thank him."

For years I have written notes to the Universe. Later, when I learned the names of my personal angels (don't ask how I know, but their names are Mark and Sheila), I would address my notes to them, always ending with: "Thanking you, in advance. Love, Betty."

Therefore, it was quite natural for me now to begin to write notes to George. Not only did I talk to him, I wrote notes. I wrote *numerous* notes. Notes of concern, notes filled with gratitude, notes of love and notes asking for his forgiveness.

Along with the notes, I often said a prayer that I had read in the book *Illuminated Prayers*, by Marianne Williamson:

"Dear God, Please sew my heart back together."

I have no idea how often I repeated that little prayer. But I do know that I said it over and over and over.

11 SIDE EFFECTS / AFFECTS OF DEATH

People react in a variety of ways to death and words of comfort cover a wide spectrum. I'm certain that no one means to say something that is construed as insensitive. Everyone does the best they know how.

Actually, we only received a handful of uncomfortable remarks. The girls didn't appreciate being asked which one of them had been their father's favorite. And I felt awful when I was told by one well-meaning woman, herself a widow, that my life was over and that no one would want to do anything with me ever again—painful words to hear when you are 56 years old. My friend, Mike, helped me sort that one out and, fortunately, the woman's prediction was totally off the mark.

The most difficult situation involved a man who would scream and yell at me that he had "lost his best friend," a "best friend" he had known for 20 years. I felt his pain. I had not only lost my best friend, but my life partner, as well.

When this person began to call me the "Widow Portenlanger," I knew that I would have to speak up and protect myself. I asked him please not to call me by that name. His reply was just as hurtful. "Well, that's what you are, you know, and you'd better get used to it."

His anger at George's death was directed at me. For almost three months, I endured his outbursts, during which time I felt sadness and also fear.

Finally, I spoke up. Never before in my life had I been talked to in that manner and I didn't intend to start letting someone treat me so cruelly at this stage of the game. I told him that I needed my energy to help myself and my daughters survive. I was very sorry for his sadness, but I couldn't help him at my expense. I wished him well and we have not spoken since.

I guess the disintegration of that "friendship" was a by-product of death. How sad. What a strange way he used to honor the memory of a "best friend."

I came to feel that George's death was indeed a multi-faceted loss.

I have one last thought to share regarding weird death comments. This is an aside to those who have never experienced the death of a spouse: please know that your first thought upon losing your partner will *not* be about how to replace that person, who is irreplaceable. Enough said on that subject.

Fortunately, the positives in what was shared with us by consoling friends far outweighed the negatives. It was amazing to experience the unexpected gifts of love that poured into our lives.

After two weeks, I returned to work. On my first day back, a father of one of my students came to see me at the end of the school day. "While we were waiting in your home to speak with you at George's visitation, we noticed that there was still a lot of painting and staining that needed to be done. We're coming over to do it for you."

"I can't ask you to do that for me," I said.

He replied, "You're not asking us to do anything. It's something that *we* need to do because of what George has meant to our children and because of what you have given to our families."

Because we had only lived in our new home for three months before George's demise, there were indeed still finishing touches that needed to be completed. *Lots* of finishing touches.

As far as I was concerned the house could stay unpainted forever. I had no energy to complete anything. Yet, these men, all Chicago firefighters, were going to take care of everything that George hadn't been able to accomplish himself. Unheard of!

Five men, over a time span of twenty days, came and worked with their hands and their hearts. It was an unbelievable gift, given without reservation and accepted with deep, deep gratitude.

Their "gift" and the effort that they needed to expend to complete the task were huge. On the final day, as I looked at their meticulous work, I could hardly voice my words of appreciation. Overcome with emotion, I did manage to thank them. They had completed the job on George's behalf, and so I thanked them for him, as well.

My sense of indebtedness was, and is, immeasurable. Tom, Steve, John, Pete, and David: to this day, when I think of these dear men, my eyes fill with tears and my heart fills with gratitude. There are no words. I love them dearly.

Our new home also needed complete landscaping. After the lawn was put in, the property had looked better, but it still needed the softening touches of flowers and bushes.

A friend from college called to say that several "old" friends were coming over to our house to put in a friendship garden. They were going to bring plants from their own yards to share with me. Then, to help complete the job, I was to make my wishes known and they would bring whatever special items I wanted from the garden center. Ten fantastic friends worked from morning 'til night, transforming my empty yard into a gorgeous garden.

How beautiful the garden! How meaningful the gift! How generous their friendship! How grateful was I!

The next week, I was looking around my home and thought, "The inside is complete and the outside is finished. All I need is a bench for the garden."

Kindergarten graduation was the following day and—lo and behold!—the afternoon class presented me with a lovely cast iron garden bench. Too wild. Too unbelievable. I had thought, "garden bench," and it had appeared.

Manifestation of thought was working at a fast pace. I was loving it, but I must admit that I was getting a bit unnerved by all of the gifts and kindnesses that were rapidly coming my way.

... and then there's my magnificent brother-in-law, Joe (George's brother). George and Joe had worked together since day one, building our new home. Not only were they brothers, but they were dear friends, too; quite a team, doing excellent work—work done to the rhythm of humorous banter and good-natured jokes.

George and I had chosen paint and wallpaper for the entire house shortly before he died. The day after his death, a call from the store notified me that the items had arrived and were ready to be picked up. Dear, dear Joe completed the whole job alone, without his co-worker. He did beautiful work, but, as he said: "It wasn't any fun without George." It was too quiet and melancholy now that half of the team was gone.

Not only did Joe complete the decorating—and several other heavy-duty tasks—but he (with the help of a forceful phone call from my friend, Fran) resolved the cosmic joke surrounding my two-year battle for an electric meter. I would like to include that story, but it is too long, too complicated, and too unbelievable. I will only allow myself to say, "What a fiasco they saw me through!"

Kate, Moll and I are so appreciative of Uncle Joe and his expertise. We're glad he is George's brother. George is glad, too.

TRIBUTES AND CONSOLATION

At the time of George's death, there were numerous personal "George Tributes" that meant a great deal to Kate, Margaret and me. The cards, letters, food, monetary contributions, and flowers were each received with appreciation.

The individual creative gifts were a marvel! It was truly remarkable that so many people would take the time to share their feelings with us.

A sincere thank you to each one!

FROM NEPHEW, MATTHEW

Our nephew, Matthew, created this poem, spontaneously, while at the family visitation. "To Uncle George" is a heartfelt remembrance filled with anguish. It is a treasure to me.

TO UNCLE GEORGE

George, I see you smiling,
Only when I close my eyes,
As I sit here crying,
Trying to say my "good-byes."
I never said, "I love you"
Or how special "Thou Art."
I will miss you forever,
From the bottom of my heart.
January 24, 2002

FROM NEPHEW, ANTHONY

Anthony, another nephew, wrote the following letter to his Uncle George. How special to have him put his thoughts into writing in a most touching way. It is another writing that I treasure.

January 24, 2002

Dear Uncle George,

Perhaps it's silly for me to write a letter to you after you've left us, but, as I think about you, I feel the need to let you know some things I really wish I could have said to you personally.

As a kid, my idea of family focused on who is married to whom and who are their children—my cousins. At some point you start to take an interest in the generation above you and what kind of people they are.

For me, the moment I saw you lighting fireworks in Grandma's backyard, you went from being my mom's older brother to something of a mythical figure. Although it might not be a compliment to some, you awakened in me the desire to light fuses and watch in awe as things blow up in a shower of sparks. I immediately understood why that would be fun, and I still do. I don't understand how some people can't relate to that. I guess some people just don't get it.

At some point, I remember my mom had been telling me about the first, and maybe only, time when she drank far too much. It was on a trip with you to New Orleans when she was 18 years old. I was really too young to know what being drunk was, but I knew that my mom was in a bad situation and I always pictured you taking care of her as she was sick. That was my only window, at the time, into your relationship with her, or with anyone, and in my head I characterized you as someone who was really loving and caring toward the important people in your life.

OK, so I did find out later that you might have played as much of a role in getting her to that point as you did in her recovery, and that you were dating her friend, but I didn't know it at the time, and I still think you were really cool for taking your little sister on a trip after her high school graduation.

It was only three or four years ago that I realized how true my characterization of you really was. Katie was coming to visit Gregory and me in New York City. I was a little worried about Katie getting into the city alone, since I had no car to pick her up, and I wrote a really long email explaining all the details, and giving her every important phone number and address I could think of. I didn't really think much of it; I was just looking out for my cousin. But when Katie arrived, she told me that you had cried or at least been really broken up at the fact that we were taking good care of your daughter.

That gave me a new view of you. I got to see a glimpse of you as a parent and I was really impressed. I've been lucky enough to get to know Katie really well over the past few years and she's become one of my very good friends. And, although I don't know Molly quite as well, we know each other better than we ever have and I enjoy spending time with both of them. Through them I've heard more stories of you and your relationship with Aunt Betty and your daughters. The love you express toward your family, and that you and Betty both share for your daughters, is really beautiful.

And now that I've been reflecting on it, I've seen glimpses of that love all along. It's the way you and Uncle Joe hang out at family gatherings, in the way you sidestep over to one of us at Christmas, cock your head to the side, and tell a joke with no intro whatsoever. Or the way you show off your latest gadgets with a childlike sense of wonder to anyone who will look.

Uncle George, your wit and your endless imagination and curiosity is an inspiration to me and I'm sure, to many others. You've left no shortage of love and great stories behind for your family, or for any of us. Unfortunately, that means there will be no shortage of tears either. But I can say that if I have any tears next Christmas when you're not there to tell me a joke or show me some new toy, you can be sure that they're going to be shed behind some multicolor snowflake glasses.

Love, Anthony

FROM NEIGHBOR, DAN

A neighbor, Dan, enjoys writing poetry. His poem, "AT NIGHT," was not originally intended to be a connection to George. In fact, he wrote it before George had died.

I have always burned "vigil"-type candles at home. Looking at the flickering flame after George's death, I would say: "Is that you, George? Are you trying to talk to me?" When I read Dan's poem, I found it eerie how the words fit in with the prevailing scheme of things; the candle and the volcano "scheme of things."

AT NIGHT

A flicker of a flame
Is Morse-candling at me.
Tinsel on a mirror.
Pulverized Glitter.
Fireflowers on a bed of gold.
A tightrope walker sprinkles
Diamonds into an active volcano
As obscure, nightly, astronomical
Moments occur: wee stars blink
Into being – flashing diatoms!
Anti-light shadows forth as a
Black gulf cradles the Moon.
Infinite cosmos wrapt in nothing.

The poem has a special meaning for me, reminding me of George's funeral wishes. Writing in a note to me, Dan agreed: "The parallels are definitely obvious. And, upon reflection, I must admit that I like the idea of diamonds as a metaphor for George's ashes, which disappear as stars come into being. It gives it a kind of mythic resonance." I marvel that it was written before his passing, yet has such a personal connection and meaning to the circumstances.

FROM GEORGE!

Two other written pieces gave me great comfort and a beautiful sense of Peace. One, that I just happened to find, was written on a little scrap of paper by George to himself. I had no idea that he had written it.

> My life is in
> God's hands. He will
> give me the wisdom
> when I need it. I just
> must ask.
> *1998*

The other piece was written by George to my mother. She shared it with me. I would like to share it with you, too, because it speaks volumes about George.

Dear Ruth,

There are a few thoughts which pass through my mind from time to time that I would like to convey to you before time slips away and they become the waste of silence.

First I would like to thank you for Betty and the superb job done in her rearing by yourself and Thomas. I consider myself very fortunate to be a part of your family as her husband. My love for her bridges to you and Thomas and I feel nothing but good toward you, now and always.

I just want you to know that you are always welcome in this home and in our company, no matter where that may be, because you are a part of us.

Sorry the jokes and wisecracks will probably continue, but always & only in good faith.

Sincerely,

George

Your son-in-law & proud of it

3-16-84

What is there to say, George? These writings are only two examples of the countless reasons why I loved you and why I will continue to love you forever. How could someone so simple and kind be so complex?

FROM NEPHEW, JEFFREY

Music seemed to play a large part in my grief and recovery process. Jeffrey, one of our nephews, composed an original musical tribute. What a gift! It is a delightfully haunting tune that goes on and on, and on and on, and then abruptly ends. Just like George's life.

FROM SISTER-IN-LAW, JOANNE

Joanne, one of my sisters-in-law, put together a CD of twelve songs she selected because each had a special meaning for me. It is a beautifully supportive and uplifting combination of music that I played repeatedly. Her gift played a large part in my healing process.

FROM FORMER NEIGHBOR, DONNA

Donna, a former neighbor, who had experienced the sudden death of her husband several years ago, stopped by with the following note and two Neil Diamond CDs:

> *Betty,*
>
> *I'm thinking of you a lot lately, knowing the difficult task you are dealing with. No one can tell you how to get thru this time, but I have certain methods that gave me temporary relief.*
>
> *I used to love to listen to all my favorite music, but found that it helped to make me feel better to have it cranked all the way up on the ol' CD player. It seemed to produce those endorphins everyone talks about.*
>
> *To enhance this effect even more, I would get on the Tri-State and crank the tunes, drive really fast, and give in to a good cry. I'd end up out at 95th Street, then turn around and come back. About an hour's investment of time—and the effect lasted several more hours after that.*
>
> *Love, Donna*

I took her advice and must admit that it worked wonders. I hadn't loved Neil Diamond before, but now I loved his music and memorized each song. I even knew the order of the songs on the CD without reading the list on the cover.

FROM 3 FRIENDS: SUE, KATHI, AND CHARLES

Three different friends, Sue, Kathi, and Charles, sent me the CD, "I Hope You Dance" by Lee Ann Womack. I would thereafter hear that particular song in the most unlikely situations. It became a sort of theme song for me. I took it to be a direct message / thought / gift from George.

Each time I would hear it play, I would smile and feel deeply loved, and offer my thanks.

The most "in your face" time that it played was when Kate and I were driving along a street in Honolulu in November of 2003. It was her birthday, and we were on the way to a little celebration on the beach. Crying, she said, "I wish Dad were here."

I said, "Turn on the radio." The announcer was giving the weather report and then a song started playing. You guessed it: the song was "I Hope You Dance." What a fabulous birthday gift from him, delivered at the precise moment of need. What I had purchased to give her as a gift paled by comparison.

The songs "To Where You Are" sung by Josh Groban, and "A Time for Farewell" sung by Cleo Laine, were also ones that I repeatedly played. The Cleo Laine song was especially beautiful music that seemed to speak to my heart and mind and soul:

> "You will be part of my heart each living moment, that's summer, come autumn, come winter come spring."

For almost 12 months straight, I would play the above-mentioned CDs over and over, and over and over. The volume was cranked up all the way, as Donna had suggested. The louder the music, the better I liked it. Is it possible to wear out a CD? I don't know about the CDs, but I had to replace the CD player.

My poor family! My poor neighbors!

I didn't care. It took a year to get that need out of my system.

At the time, I had no knowledge of the word "entrainment." I would later learn that my inner distress mirrored the volume of and choice of the music I was playing. These outer sounds matched my inner feelings. I was *entrained* with the selections. In time, as I calmed down inside, the volume calmed down as well.

I must admit that I had become quite familiar with the loudness, and I missed it, as I had rather come to love it. But I just didn't need it anymore. I had turned a corner.

FROM FRIEND, TOM

A friend, Tom, shared some tapes on grieving that had helped him survive the untimely death of his first wife. He, along with Mike, another friend, and Mary, my sister-in-law, knew firsthand the unbearable anguish I was experiencing. They helped in ways that only those who have been in the same, sad place could perfectly understand.
But these dear people had also had the added sorrow of being left to raise young children on their own. How had they traveled this route? How had they managed? I relived their pain as well as my own.

FROM FRIEND, KATHI

And then there was Kathi, who repeatedly called, brought lunch, and watched in total amazement as my daughters and I would engage in wild verbal and, sometimes, physical behavior, all in an effort to survive. She never betrayed our antics, probably because she was at a loss as to how to describe the scene. A true friend ...

FROM GEORGE'S SISTER, MARY

George's sister, Mary, made pins for Kate, Moll, me and each of George's siblings; each was a black ribbon with a token symbolizing a personal connection to George. Mine had a heart and an anchor with the words: "brokenhearted, but anchored in his love." Kate's had the word "Dad" written on it, and Moll's had "Papa." How special for each of us.
George had once commented to Mary that, in the movie, "It's A Wonderful Life," when Mr. Bailey died, his son wore a black arm band.
George had thought it showed respect. In mourning, and out of respect for her brother, Mary made these tributes for each of us to wear.

FROM GEORGE'S BROTHER, JOHN AND FAMILY

John, George's brother, along with his wife, Joann, and their daughter, Jenna, gave us a beautiful plaque: "This house was built with love by George Portenlanger."
How meaningful, especially now. George certainly had put his heart and soul and love into every corner!

FROM NEIGHBOR, KRIS

Along with music, books played a major part in my healing. One day, I opened my door to find several books from my neighbor, Kris. I credit her with starting me on my path toward a deeper understanding.
She introduced me to literature that expanded my horizons. The first book I read was *Journey of Souls* by Michael Newton.
Other readings that spoke to my heart were:

- *Anam Cara*, by John O'Donohue
- *I Heard God Laughing*, by Daniel Ladinsky and
- *Death of a Husband*, by Helen Reickert Lamben

During the two years after George's death, I read twenty-nine books in an attempt to help myself figure out what was taking place. My mind was being expanded in many new directions, new dimensions, and new horizons that I had never heard of previously.
But I bet that George had known all about these ideas. I never would have listened to him before, but he had my complete attention now.
A listing of my readings can be found at the end of this book in the Addenda section.

There is no way that I can ever repay the countless people who, quietly and unassumingly, came forward to share in our grief; to help us in innumerable ways.

I wrote personal thank you notes to all of our family and friends. On the cover of each note, I had printed a sort of quote that I thought epitomized what George might have said:

> *When I entered this life,*
> *I cried and you rejoiced.*
> *When I exited this life,*
> *I rejoiced and you cried.*

To everyone who cried along with us and shared our grief, I can only say: you have no idea how much your support meant. May you and your loved ones receive untold blessings in return.

13 LOIS AND CAROL

Several days after George's death, I was talking by phone with my friend, Lois. Lois now lives in California, but it was my good fortune to meet her in college at Northern Illinois University.

There is absolutely no way for me to describe Lois. A friend of hers in Hawaii has called her, simply "an amazing woman." There's no doubt about it; she certainly is that.

In this lifetime, Lois has been given many gifts. And in return, Lois has, herself, been a gift to many. Her energy, humor, kindness, enthusiasm for living, and talents are enormous.

During the course of this particular phone conversation, it came up how we, in George's family, had held three types of local "services" for George. However, we still had to figure out how we would take care of his wish to be thrown into a volcano.

Without missing a beat, Lois said, "I know the answer!" Lois, it happens, is quite familiar with the big island of Hawaii, and she knew all about the Kilauea volcano, located in the Hawai'i Volcanoes National Park on that island.

"Kilauea is an active volcano, and it would be perfect!" she said. "We can all travel together to the island and complete the journey for George."

"Lois, I can't accept that from you," I said. I didn't want to risk inconveniencing her in any way.

"Of course you can," she replied, "you and Kate and Molly *must* come!"

"Thank you, Lois … I'll think about it … "

Hanging up the phone, I was engulfed with a feeling of excitement and promise. Kate and Margaret afterwards wondered what I had needed to think about. How could I not have said "yes" instantly? This was too unbelievable!

Before that phone call, I had had no idea of how I was going to figure out the volcano angle.

But, after the phone call, it was all taken care of. That was pretty good!

Thank you, to whomever was making this all work.

Lois called me the next day and I accepted her gracious offer. Although it was only February and we wouldn't be going until August, planning for and thinking about the trip gave us something to look forward to. Kate, Moll and I were filled with excitement in the midst of our grieving.

The promise of the volcano wasn't the only priceless gift of hope I received from Lois. Two-and-a-half weeks after George died, she again called and said, "There's someone I'd like you to talk with."

It was then that I first met, by way of phone, Carol Dirck. The date was February 9, 2002.

As difficult as it is for me to describe Lois, it's equally as difficult to describe Carol. Her business card reads: "Intuitive Counseling, Focused on the Mind, Body and Spirit Connection." She does spiritual counseling and motivational speaking. I simply call her "my bridge." I have no idea how she does it, but she has been gifted with the ability to connect with a higher realm. Carol is a devout Catholic and deeply spiritual. She uses her gift in a supportive, kind and loving way, always for the greater good.

Carol explained to me that, at the time of the car accident, George had not been speaking to *me* when he said, "Help me. Please help…"

She said, "I feel that he took great care of you during his life and, realizing that he was now leaving his body, he knew that you were going to be involved in an accident. He was asking the One who was coming to meet him for help, so that you would not be hurt."

Exactly! Her explanation made perfect sense. That's exactly what happened.

If I hadn't been in the car, if I hadn't been in the back seat, I wouldn't have been in the unique situation to both see and hear the whole event. The way he looked up slightly to the left, the softness of his voice—the exact what-and-how of its happening—these made her explanation perfect. George hadn't been speaking to

me. He had been speaking to someone *he* could see but *I couldn't*. Why hadn't I thought of that?
Carol and I talked at length, for about an hour and a half. Actually, she talked and I cried, then we talked and I cried some more. I was both amazed and comforted by what she said.
She and I didn't know one another; we had never met. She had never known George; she had no idea where I lived or who I was. But she knew things. She knew concrete and personal things.
I was confused when she told me that there was a problem in my kitchen. Water was dripping through an area that had not been sealed; extra caulking needed to be done. Since cooking is not one of my loves, I'm not in the kitchen for long periods of time. Therefore, I hadn't noticed anything.
"George wants you to know it's easy to fix. Just ask the firemen, or his brother, Joe," she said.
How could Carol possibly have known about the firemen or Joe, let alone the caulking that needed to be done in my kitchen?
I didn't even know about the problem. She had never been in my home; neither had Lois, so Lois couldn't have mentioned it to her. And, while Lois knew George, she had no knowledge of the firemen.
Quite interesting ...
Even though I lived in our house, I had no clue as to what she was referring. I thought the missing caulking must be where the countertop meets the wall. It wasn't until almost a month after our conversation that I even found the problem. It wasn't at the wall. It was caulking that was needed to seal a portion of the sink itself.
I asked Joe for help. It was easy to fix; just a small problem that had the potential to turn into a big problem had it gone unnoticed. I thanked Joe, and I also thanked George.
One more thing that amazed me about Carol was how did she know, when I was sitting alone in Chicago, and she was sitting in California, with our talking to one another for the first time, such a specific thing as that I was wearing George's comforting cap (his Irish cap that is such a source of comfort to me)?

Would I have told anyone that information? No; it was private. But she knew. I hadn't told her. *He* had told her. I loved it! After living with George for 33 years and from all the reading I was now doing, and from this conversation with Carol, I was beginning to understand.

But understand what?

Hanging up the phone, I sat there, silently looking around the room. I appeared to be alone, but I knew I wasn't alone. This was weird. This was dumb. This wasn't real. I couldn't tell too many people about this. Everyone would have a rational explanation for all that had just transpired. The only thing that I knew for certain was that there *was* no rational explanation!

This wasn't wishful thinking. This wasn't a phony baloney deal. This wasn't Satan. Lois wasn't feeding Carol information about certain specific situations that had taken place in my life. Lois had no way of knowing such things anyway! The only one who had been with me, and in on these certain specific situations, was *George*.

He was the one who was feeding her the information.

I wanted to know just one thing: I wanted to know just how this all worked ...

All along, George had been right when he said: "We are made up of incredible energy. Energy cannot be destroyed; it can only change." His energy had changed. Mine had not. His way of knowing had expanded. I was doing my best to expand as well. However, my energy was stuck in the confines of my own limitations, my own earthly limitations.

In thinking about the dramatic shift in the direction of my life, my new house became a symbol of that new life. I am a visual learner, and this was an up-close-and-visual lesson.

Suddenly, I could see that the move from our old house to our new house graphically described the change that had taken place with George. When we moved, we still lived on the exact same piece of property, but we had a totally different view; a totally different vantage point from which to see our same surroundings. We had lived here for 30 years, but now we were looking at things from a new angle, a new dimension. Same piece of property, totally different perspective.

So, too, with George.

Same George. Same soul. Different view. Different vantage point. Different perspective.

Dr. Wayne Dyer has said, "When you change the way you look at things, the things you look at change."

But I didn't even know what I was *looking* at, so how would I be able to *change* that view, *my* view? This was totally out of my range of vision and, most certainly, all out of focus.

Carol knew how to change the way she looked at things. She knew how to adjust the viewfinder. I wanted to be able to do what she could do. I wanted to eliminate the middle man. With every fiber of my being I wished that I could crack the code!

I have since grown to call Carol my friend as well as my bridge. I marvel at her ability. How fortunate for me that she came into my life. Knowing her has made all the difference in the world to me; all the difference in my world, George's world, and the joining of the two.

SOLO TO OAHU

It was June, 2002. School was out for the summer. The events of the last five months had left me exhausted.

On the spur of the moment, I decided to go to Hawaii. In August, I would be going with Kate and Moll. But now, for mental health purposes, I felt I couldn't wait. I needed to go right then.

This was to be the first of ten trips that I would take in a two-year time frame; eight trips to the Hawaiian Islands and two to a favorite place in Key West.

A bit of travel excess, if you ask me. But I gave myself permission anyway. I felt the need to be renewed by a spiritual presence, quiet solitude, and glorious nature.

My friend, Charles, made it easier to go. A friend whom I have known since high school, he has lived on Oahu since the '60s. Shortly after George's death, he had sent his condolences, along with a book on the volcanoes of Hawaii. In the first few months, in the midst of my grief, he was a tremendous help. It was comforting to have a friend of long standing listen to my crying and lend supportive words of care and consolation.

Since I wasn't used to traveling alone, I thought it would be safest to travel to a place where I would at least know someone.

Staying by myself, on Kalakaua Avenue in Honolulu, I was able to enjoy the luxury of solitude in the midst of the bustle of Waikiki. The stay proved to be just what I needed. It did wonders for my heart, mind and soul.

During my stay, I received three noteworthy gifts:

The *first*: Chuck introduced me to Alice. Alice owns three delightful homes, located directly on the beach in Waimanalo. She is someone with whom I instantly felt a true kinship.

I had come five months into this new life. Crying, I asked Alice, herself a widow, if I would ever be happy again.

"Take a walk on the beach by yourself, dear, and you will find comfort in the beauty. Simply listen."

To this very day, her beach and her kindness have a special healing meaning for me.

Even though we now don't see one another often, I consider Alice to be a dear friend. I feel as if I have known her forever. She is another gift from the heavens; a gift given to me at precisely my exact moment of need.

The *second* "gift" experience of note took place during a morning ocean swim. I had been agonizing about what I should do with regard to my five wedding rings. It's a long story, but, yes, there are five: three are mine and two are George's. They are all from our single marriage. Each one of them had a very special meaning to me.

The most recent one that I was wearing was George's, the one that I had taken from his finger in the hospital and put on my finger. How could I ever take it off? *Why* would I ever take it off?

As far as I was concerned, I wanted to keep wearing them. However, I had noticed that others who were newly widowed, had removed their rings. I had no idea regarding the protocol of rings once your partner was deceased.

That morning, floating in the beautiful water, the answer came to me ever so clearly: I never had to take them off! I could wear them forever if I so chose; an obvious answer. This was totally a non-issue that I had made into a huge cause of concern; now it was a cause for concern no longer. I could do exactly as I wanted, and I wanted to keep wearing my rings, all five of them on one finger. I kept on floating and said, "Thank you!"

The *third* experience boggles my mind to this very day. I was positively thrilled by it but completely startled as well, and more than a bit unnerved. George always loved the Fourth of July and delighted in setting off fireworks. I did not share his enthusiasm for exploding things.

Alone in my hotel room, I was getting ready to go to a picnic in Kapiolani Park. It was the Fourth of July 2002. I was almost ready to leave the room when the most incredible thing happened:

I could *see* it, but it wasn't visible.

I could *hear* it, but it didn't make a sound.
I could *feel* it, but I didn't touch it.
"It" was shaped like a tornado, and my body shook, as it blended into me from my feet up.
I stood there, somewhat frozen in place.
The whole experience lasted little more than an instant, but it is something that will remain with me forever.
It was just like Whoopi Goldberg in the movie *Ghost*.
I had no doubt who "It" was.
Out loud, I said, "George, how did you do that?"
I absolutely loved it! Of course, I knew it was George. Who or what else could it have been? And, could you blame him? He wanted to go to the Fourth of July picnic, too.
"Let's go!" I said, and we went to the festivities together.
But I'm asking you, how do you think he did it? I'd still like to know. I'd really still like to know.
Actually, I'd really like to have him do that trick again. It was pretty good!

Completely re-energized, I went home at the end of the week, knowing that I would be returning to Hawaii again the next month.
Though it seemed somewhat bizarre and out of this world, I was traveling with George.
Traveling with George and loving it.
Another "Thank you" was in order!

THE VOLCANO OF KILAUEA

That August, I again went to Hawaii, this time on a sacred mission. And, to prepare for the trip, I had a special errand to fulfill ...

Kate had gone with me, that day, but waited in the car, when I went to the funeral home to get George's ashes. George had always shown an aversion similar to Kate's, never liking to sit down or eat any food in funeral homes.

I stepped inside the "home." The woman funeral director greeted me and told me to have a seat while she went to get "George."

I sat down and waited, thinking of George for all kinds of reasons ...

... (at least I wasn't eating anything) ...

The woman reappeared, carrying a canvas sack trimmed with rainbow handles. I looked into the sack and saw that the box with his ashes was inside.

"So, it's come to this," I thought. "I'm carrying him around in a bag with rainbow handles. Am I really experiencing this?"

The woman asked, "Would you prefer to use the service entrance on your way out?"

"No, thank you," I replied. "We'll go out the front door."

Carrying the heavy sack, walking down the outside front steps, I hoped that I didn't trip and throw him all over Northwest Highway. That would have been awful. Perhaps the service entrance had been a good suggestion.

Arriving at the car, I asked Kate if she wanted to see her father.

"Just get in and let's go!" was her response.

I put George in the back seat (no seat belt).

Once at home, I told the girls, "If anyone wants to know how your father is doing, tell them he's at home, resting comfortably."

They didn't respond.

Later, I stood in front of the television, holding "the box."

"What are you doing?" asked the girls.
"He's standing in front of the TV, like he always did!"
"Not funny, Mom."
George would have thought it was funny.
They didn't.
Actually, I didn't think it was funny either.
This whole "joke" had gone on long enough! It could end any time now, as far as I was concerned. It was as if someone were playing a game and had called out, "Red Rover, Red Rover, let George come over." Then he'd crossed over, gone in an instant.

But I'd had enough of the game, and wanted to shout "Come out, come out wherever you are!" I was hoping he would come walking into the room.

That wasn't about to happen.

Now that we had the ashes, we were ready to fulfill George's request with the arrival of August.

I decided that I couldn't throw all of George into the volcano. It was too far from home. I would only take a small portion out there.

The girls and I decided that we would each write a note to him, and each would choose a shirt of his to take along. Once we reached Hawaii, we would have a bonfire on the beach, burning the shirts and the notes. Mixing George's ashes with the ashes from our memorial fire, we would then carry them with us in our journey onward to Kilauea.

A few days before we were to leave, I stopped at my neighbor, Sue's, for a visit. She had a new deck of "Goddess" cards. Forty-eight cards represented a variety of Goddesses from various types of feminine mythology: Greek, Roman, Celtic, Native American, Egyptian, Middle Eastern, and Scandinavian.

"Shuffle the cards and pick one," she said to me.

I shuffled the cards and chose. I had selected Pele, the fiery Hawaiian volcano Goddess.

Of all the cards, Pele emerged! How perfect! How foretelling! I knew we would have a safe and exciting journey.

I carried the Pele card on the entire trip, even across the lava field. It was wonderful to have her traveling with us.

Never having known anyone who was cremated, and particularly because this involved George, I wasn't certain if I would be able, from a mental standpoint, to open the container of ashes.

When it was time, my neighbor, Marty, offered his services and, gratefully, I accepted his kindness.

Standing in my kitchen, Marty opened the container.

I looked in at the contents. "So, that's what ashes look like!" I thought.

I think I then said something trite, like "ashes to ashes and dust to dust." I look back on the moment with regret. Here I was, looking at what, to me, was sacred, and all I could come up with was a cliché.

For handling purposes, we decided to use the Delta Airlines spoon that George had lifted years ago during one of our trips.

We also decided that a baker's dozen of scoops would be sufficient.

To know Marty is to love him. Marty is a "character" in every good and positive sense of that term. He is also, with his family, a kind and generous next-door neighbor. He was the perfect person to help me with this undertaking; truly the *perfect* person.

With everything in place, we were ready to fly.

Well, not quite. A slight mix-up at the airport regarding the correct spelling of Kate's given name was cause for considerable angst. After I began to cry, saying that we simply *had* to "get on this plane so that we could bury my dead husband" (as if we would bury my live husband), all was resolved. We were on our way.

Upon arriving in Kona, we (Kate, Moll and I) were met by Lois.

At the end of the little airport road, we had to stop at one of the few traffic lights on the island.

"Lois!" I said, "Check out that car!"

On the side of the road sat an empty car. No one was around, inside or out. We were the only ones on the road.

The license plate on the car had three letters and no numbers on it. The letters were GFP. George Francis Portenlanger. We were four speechless women looking at that empty car. It was as if he were welcoming us to the island.

Did we love it? You know we did. It was too, too wild.

For the rest of that trip, and on subsequent visits to the Big Island, I have looked for that car. I've never spotted it. In fact, I have found that almost all of the license plates on that particular island begin with the letter H, representing the island of Hawaii.

That night, we went down to watch the sunset while having some drinks and appetizers at The Beach Bar. Afterwards, we were going to have our bonfire ceremony on the beach ...

In the midst of this gorgeous setting, I kept wondering how we were going to collect and carry the ashes from our bonfire.

I was annoyed at myself for not figuring out this very important part. Why hadn't I planned ahead?

We ordered appetizers, which included French fries. The fries arrived at our table, served in a brass bucket, complete with carrying handle. Lois and I had the exact, same thought: what a perfect vessel for our mission!

We finished our drinks and food, watched the sunset, asked permission to keep the bucket, and set off on our journey to the beach.

There had been no need for me to be concerned about a container for the hot ashes. Once again, a solution had arrived with precise timing ... and I hadn't done a thing. All I needed to do was say "Thank you."

Lois had arranged everything for our ceremony for George. A dear friend of hers carried out the bonfire handling part perfectly. His skills were amazing, as he brought our fire to a blaze. George, always known as the Rambo of Fireworks, would have thoroughly approved.

We ceremoniously laid our notes and George's beloved shirts onto the fire, toasting our memories of him with champagne under a gorgeous, starry sky. It was a perfect setting. The only imperfection was that we had to do it at all.

Then, gathering up the hot embers and ashes, we carried the now-untouchably-hot bucket on a stick we had found.

It was late; we needed to head home. Tomorrow would be a long day, and we would have to get an early start.

We left the next morning for the two-and-a-half hour drive to the Chain of Craters Road that was in Hawai'i Volcanoes National Park on the other side of the island.

As we began our journey, a little gecko crawled up the hood of the car and affixed himself to the passenger side of the windshield. Hanging on for dear life, he rode along until lunchtime.

When we stopped to eat, he crawled under the hood to rest. We thought he was gone, but as we started up to complete the trip, he crawled back to his place on the windshield. Once again, he hung on for dear life until we reached our destination.

At last we were inside the park. As if he knew that he had arrived, the gecko released his toes and flung himself off into the volcanic rock. Having escorted us the entire trip, his job was now complete.

Quite symbolic ...

As luck would have it, the volcano of Kilauea was erupting big time! It was a sight to behold!

We walked about two miles across hot rocks to see the red molten lava, pouring into the ocean.

All the other hikers present were properly prepared for their walk across these extensive lava fields. They wore hiking boots and carried water bottles.

Never having done this before, the four of us had on our sandals. I was the only one for miles around who was wearing a dress and carrying a huge purse. I have no clue what I had been thinking in preparing for this trek.

But I knew what I was thinking now:

> *George, I don't think you had any idea what you were asking us to do when you made your original volcano wish. You certainly have taken us on a grand adventure.*

The sight around us was dramatic and magnificent. Our lack of hiking gear didn't matter; we were on a mission.

As we walked over the first lava field we had come to, we decided that it was too crowded and too public for having our private ceremony.

So, we got back in the car and drove a short distance to a quiet area. There, Lois stopped the car, and Kate, Moll, Lois and I got out ... I then walked down onto the lava with the bucket, and lovingly scattered the ashes over what had now become an Altar of Nature. Aloud, I read the following words:

> Georgie—You fulfilled your sacred agreement with the Universe. We were honored and delighted to travel with you through this lifetime. You were loving, and dearly loved. The lessons that you taught us, the incredible laughs and fun we shared, and the beautiful life you allowed us to lead, will never be forgotten by us.
>
> Thank you for connecting with us in this lifetime and thank you for continuing to connect with and to care for us.
>
> Your spirit, soul and love are awesome and a treasure to us!
>
> We symbolically scatter your earthly body in joyous celebration of the life we shared. Cat Stevens said "you only dance on this earth for a short while." We were blessed to be your partner.
>
> Thank you, George. We will meet and travel together again.
>
> I love you. You are my Anam Cara.[1]
>
> Betty
>
> August 4, 2002
>
> 1:00 PM Kilauea Volcano

---

[1] *Anam Cara* is Gaelic for "soul friend" and the name of a book by John O'Donohue. It is pronounced "AH-nam KAH-ra."

The setting was spectacular: the volcano, the ocean, and the expansive sky.

I had accomplished my task, accomplished it for George.

Turning around, I looked up to see Lois, Moll and Kate in tears. I had been too focused on finding the "perfect" spot and completing the reading to cry.

Seeing them, I was reminded of just why I was standing there.

My time for tears then came.

The four of us, together crying, again toasted George with champagne. I didn't drink all of mine. I walked back to George and poured the last of my glass onto his memorial.

"Here's to you, Georgie. I love you. May God rest your soul."

16 THE FINALE

Because we wanted family and friends to be a part of the ceremony at the volcano, I had sent the following letter in advance of our trip, to people I felt would want to be included. In that way, even though the ocean and a great distance separated us physically, we could join together in our love for George.

In this effort to have a collective gathering, I wrote:

> *Dear Family and Friends,*
>
> *Kate, Margaret and I are leaving for Hawaii on July 31. We are staying in San Francisco for two days and leaving for Kona on August 2. The purpose of our trip is to fulfill George's wish. The journey that we are taking for George is a sad and difficult one for us.*
>
> *I am writing to let you know that on Sunday, August 4, at 1:00 PM Hawaii time (6:00 PM Chicago time), we will gather to symbolically (and, in part, physically) commit George's earthly body to the Kilauea Volcano.*
>
> *I have enclosed the words that I will read at this ceremony. It is our hope that you will join with us at this time in a united thanksgiving to God and to the Universe for our dear George. We will feel your support and will thereby receive strength to complete our task.*
>
> *Thank you for being there with us. And, thank you for being there for George—for our dear, unique George.*
>
> *Love, Betty*
>
> *July 2002*

I later returned home from Hawaii to find numerous notes and calls from family and friends.

Each wanted to explain how they had joined together with us in thought and spirit at the volcano. It was heart-warming to know that, even though we had been miles away, we had been linked together as one with those close to home.

Jeanine's e-mail echoed the thoughts of many. It truly had been a gathering of minds for George.

Subj: A Toast for George

Date: 08/04/02 9:56:19 PM Central Daylight Time

Betty,

At 6 o'clock Chicago time, I thought of you, Kate, Molly and George. So I raised my beer glass to George and to all of the kindness, love and knowledge that he projected into the world. Cheers!

Love, Jeanine

The Hawaiian volcano mission had been accomplished.
That part of my life was now completed.

George and I, throughout our years together, had always made travel arrangements with the help of Jim and Mike O'Malley, our wonderful travel agents at Diplomat Travel.

91

Mike was fond of calling George "the Gentle Giant," and Jim enjoyed sharing jokes with George as itineraries were being arranged.

The year continued on. With the help of the dear O'Malleys, so did I. In order to cope, I traveled.

George traveled, too. He is scattered in numerous places:
- all over the Hawaiian Islands
- at Key West
- in the Pacific Ocean
- at Lake Tahoe, and
- at McCormick Place

to name a few locations. He is shared with the volcano, the land, and the ocean.

After I scattered some ashes in a very public fountain, I found out that ashes do not dissolve in water. They don't dissolve; they spread.

Poor Kate was with me.

"This time you've gone too far, Mom!" she said, as we ran from the scene.

Shortly after George died, I was passing the intersection of Halsted and Diversey and saw the *Streetwise* newspaper salesman who had comforted me. Whenever I find myself at the exact place of George's death, I make the sign of the cross, and say, "God rest your soul, George."

This time, because I had spotted the man, I stopped my car, and went to thank him for his help that night and to give him a monetary remembrance.

When I walked up to him, I said, "I don't know if you remember me ... "

"Of course I do! How's he doing?"

I explained that George had died, but that I wanted him to

know how much his kindness had meant to me that day and how I would never forget him.

Connecting with this man and being able to thank him personally made me feel that I had completed another portion of my task.

A year went by before I would be able to complete my entire agenda ...

It was now the first year anniversary of George's death, January 21, 2003.

Kate, Margaret and I took the day off from our respective jobs. During the day, we went back to the hospital and the fire station. I needed to thank the people who had been so helpful and kind in that impossible situation the previous year.

Taking bagels, cream cheese, and coffee to them didn't quite equal the magnitude of their attention to us, but it was a heartfelt thank-you on my part. Everyone was most grateful for the treats, but their gratitude could never come close to the appreciation and love I felt for these dedicated people.

That evening we held a GEORGE FEST.

It was a way of remembering George, a somewhat small gathering in honor of the dear man.

GEO♥RGE FEST
2003

WHAT: an open house
WHERE: the Portenlanger Home
WHEN: Tuesday, January 21
WHY: To remember George and celebrate the man and the myth

Please join us.

Betty, Katie and Molly

Since no one had ever been to a "George Fest" before, the celebration was unique and somewhat subdued.

At 7:00 PM, I lit a candle, shut off the lights and said, "George, last year at this very moment we were standing in the street. This year, we honor your memory. Send us a sign, so that we know you are here with us."

At that very moment, the doorbell rang.

We all screamed!

It was my cousin and her family.

Actually, I know it was George. He just used Terry as the vehicle to ring the bell so that he could say hello. Wild, perfect timing!

The year had come full circle. We had tried our best to honor, celebrate and remember. I think George would have been pleased with our efforts. Our outward journey of mourning was complete.

But the inward journey of love will continue forever ...

PART FOUR:
CONNECTING

17 FOR YOUR CONSIDERATION ...

The following section contains information and ideas that may not be suitable for more sensitive and/or predisposed readers. It contains ideas that may be distressing to some.

The author does not wish to offend anyone. It is her truth. It may not be your truth, but it is just as valid. Mutual respect is all she asks. She suggests that there is value in her thoughts and opinions, even though they may differ from those of the reader.

Please know that she values your truth and sincerely hopes that you are at peace with your path. We are all enlightened.

Just as there are a myriad number of ways to arrive at the number 12:

10+2, 15-3, 1+11, 6+6, 9+3, 41-29, 608-596, 5+7, *ad infinitum*, so too are there various ways to arrive at the truth.

I hope that you will enjoy this next section. Please read it with an open mind and an open heart.

18 CONNECTING

Throughout my life, I have asked, at times, "What is this *(i.e., life)* all about? What are we supposed to be doing?"

Previously, I had only wondered. Now, I had absolutely *no* clue.

I was, however, determined to figure it out. I wanted to put the puzzle pieces together so I could solve the one huge question in my mind: *How can I stay connected to George's energy?*

It's difficult to solve a mystery. It's especially difficult when you have no idea where to begin or in what direction you are actually heading.

There were a few things I did that helped me immensely, though.

So, I am going to share my ideas with you.

Because the results were so exciting, I feel I would be wrong to keep my discoveries a secret. In fact, I feel as if I am guided to share them.

It is just like when you find a new product that you like, or a new use for an old product, and you want to share your discovery with your family and friends.

I feel *compelled* to share my life discoveries with you; I need to let others in on the information. To do otherwise would be selfish.

Please keep in mind that, if you were telling me these things, I would secretly think that you were totally off-balance, in need of heavy medication, and/or totally delusional.

The rational side of my brain tells me that these things aren't for real. The other part of my brain tells me, "You saw it happen. How can you deny what just took place?"

It is confusing, upsetting, exciting and comforting, all at the same time.

Feeling that I am pretty mainstream in my beliefs, I do not want others to view me as someone who is "way out there."

But, since George's death, I have experienced some very

unusual happenings. At times, I think that I am living in a Harry Potter-like realm.

I am very aware that there is a Higher Power involved in my life. However, my experiences are difficult to explain and I certainly have no idea as to how this all works. As I watch the unfolding of my life, as I now know it, I can only wonder ...

... I am in awe ...

As an introverted extrovert, I want to tell everyone and, at the same time, to tell no one. Therefore, I am quite selective about the people with whom I share my information. When I do share, I can get quite passionate about the subject. Afterwards, I get embarrassed about my boldness, and have the need to hibernate for a while. It is as if I have invaded my own privacy and exposed a part of myself that is vulnerable, precious and inestimable.

But, if you are interested, I am willing to risk derision in order to help you connect with those no longer physically present whom you dearly love.

Perhaps you have ways that you already know and feel comfortable using. I will tell you what I did to help myself and, if you choose, you may use my ideas along with your own. It is my hope that you will have the same, if not greater, success.

You will, perhaps, feel strange and silly in trying these ideas, but if you have a deep desire for this process to work and a deep sense of knowing that it *will* work, then you will break down the negative barriers in your mind.

I suggest that you may want to do your "research" in private. May I also suggest that, at first, you share the exciting results only with trusted, interested and like-minded individuals. Otherwise, you may meet with ridicule that will cause you to doubt yourself and your sanity.

Don't quit. If you do, you will miss the desired end-result: *Connecting*.

I am a common, normal, everyday individual, who has experienced unusual, exceptional and remarkable happenings.

If I can experience it, you can, too. You simply have to open your mind to new possibilities.

As it says in the book, *Tuesdays With Morrie,* "Death ends a life, not a relationship."
If you are interested in continuing your relationship with your departed loved ones, what do you have to lose? Nothing. What do you have to gain? Everything!

I've mentioned elsewhere that, after George died, I began my book-reading marathon.
One day, about eight months into the readings, I was at a book store and happened to find myself in the "Spiritual" section.
One book seemed to simply "be there." It didn't fall off the shelf, but it was "there" and it got my attention.
I leafed through it and put it back on the shelf. After browsing through several other books, I returned to the first book because, at this point, it *had* fallen off the shelf.

RULE #1: There are no coincidences. Heads up!
Learn to read the signs in your life.

So, I figured that this book was being brought to my attention for a particular reason. Perhaps I had better check it out once more.
I opened to a page that had to do with pendulum dowsing. I had been familiar with the idea of pendulums ever since the time of my sister's kidnap and murder, many years ago.
Jeannie was missing, and presumed dead, but the police were unable to locate her body. After three days, a woman, named Helen Beamsley, was brought in to help with the search. Using a pendulum, Mrs. Beamsley was instrumental in assisting the police in locating my sister's body.
At that time, when I would relate the story of how my sister was found, I remember people being extremely skeptical.
How could it be? The woman had to have been in on the murder. How could she possibly have known so much information unless she was somehow involved?

This woman had, of course, absolutely nothing to do with my sister's disappearance and death. But she did, however, have a great deal to do with finding the location of, and expediting the recovery of, her body.

I had no idea how pendulum dowsing worked. All I knew was that my sister had been found and that I was extremely grateful to Mrs. Beamsley.

Fast forward to the bookstore and the book falling off the shelf. I purchased the book, took it home, and read the part about dowsing several times.

It seems that pendulums are a way of using energy. They have been used to answer questions since the first century. They were in use during the Roman Empire.

You will have to do further research on your own if you want to find out in-depth information on pendulum dowsing. Pendulums are sold in stores, but you can make one yourself.

I will give you a quick idea of how dowsing works:

A small weight is attached to a chain (you can use a necklace chain) or cord. Hold the chain in your hand, between your thumb and index finger, to allow the pendulum to swing freely.

First you must determine your "personal directions." While holding the pendulum, ask to be shown which way is "Yes." The pendulum will then move either back and forth or from side to side.

Then ask to be shown which way is "No." Again, the pendulum will move, but in the opposite direction from the previous answer.

After asking to be shown your personal directions, and establishing them, you are good to go. Ask your question, and the pendulum will respond. You may ask your questions out loud, or silently, in your mind. Either way will work.

Now, back to my book purchase: as I said, I returned home and began to read the book. I found it fascinating and I wanted to try the technique for myself. Since it was quite late at night at this point, and no stores were open, I decided to make my own pendulum, using something that contained George's energy.

I went down into the basement and looked through his electrical material. I found the perfect items: I chose three metal washers—one large, and two of a smaller size. They were perfect, because each had a hole in the center, through which I could string the chain.

The smaller washers I put on either side of the larger one. Perfect. I had made a personalized pendulum; personalized with George's own belongings.

I couldn't wait to see if it would work.

Sitting alone in my kitchen, becoming even more excited, I now had no doubt that it would work. I tried it out.

I wasn't disappointed; I was ecstatic. I felt connected. I was alone, but totally connected.

Connected to what? Connected to whom? I didn't know. It was wild ...

Knowing that I couldn't share this with too many people, I shared it with Kate and Moll a few days later.

I said, "Check this out; you won't believe it. Go ahead and ask a question."

Kate and Moll began protesting almost at once. Words flew back and forth.

"You're moving your hand to make it move."

"No, I'm not."

"Yes, you are."

"I am not."

Kate said, "Please don't show this to too many people. They will think that you are completely strange and won't understand."

She was right. I wouldn't understand if someone had shown it to me. I wouldn't have understood it, or believed it, or even cared.

But this was *my* connection and it was for *me*, so I believed and I cared.

It's just that I didn't *understand*. I *still* don't understand. I only know that if George were standing here he could explain the entire concept.

Since I don't believe that George is a sideshow, or a parlor trick, I have been quite selective about showing this technique to people. When I did share this "secret," these were the results:

- two people were totally freaked by it
- one person said I was going over the edge, that this was the work of the Devil, and reported me to his priest
  and
- the rest are as fascinated and comforted by the pendulum movement as am I.

The most interesting outcome has been the number of times people have called me on the phone or come in person, wanting to "ask George a question." I love it that there are those who view it as I do—a valid, legitimate, real method of uniting with spirit.

There have been times when I have asked a question, wanting a specific response, and was surprised and annoyed that the pendulum didn't give me the answer that I wanted. So I would repeatedly ask the same question, even trying to swing it in the direction I desired. The answer never changed, no matter how hard I would try to "think" it into a different direction.

I have no idea how the pendulum moves, but I know that it has something to do with energy, the energy of which we are all made, just as George talked about. I only know that it moves and that I can elicit eight different responses:

1. yes
2. no
3. diagonal (the diagonal slash direction indicated by the universal sign for "no")
4. clockwise circle
5. counterclockwise circle
6. no movement
7. direct contact (where the pendulum moves over and touches my arm) and
8. instantaneous stopping.

Each movement represents a specific meaning.

This testing can be rather unnerving to view, so I rarely use the pendulum when others are present. Actually, I don't care to leave myself open to ridicule, so I seldom choose to share this process with anyone when I'm using it, not even Kate and Moll.

Though I have made one of these pendulums for each of the girls, I view doing the actual process as sacred, beautiful, and comforting beyond belief. To me, it is private, confidential and intensely personal. A direct connection. Quite powerful.

I have encouraged two other people, who were not family members, to use my pendulum. It is interesting to note that both of them found it to be an extremely emotional experience. Each had to get past an initial rush of tears before continuing on with their questions.

While I do not do it often, I find that it is a forceful phenomenon, not only to personally experience, but to view, as well.

One day, a colleague, Maureen, brought some family pictures to school. She asked me to look at them and tell her if I noticed anything unusual about the pictures.

Each of the pictures, where her son or daughter was present, had an additional marking on it: a perfect little circle appeared on each of the pictures. It looked like a little smiley face without the facial features.

On each of the pictures, the marking appeared in a different location. Therefore, it could not have been a fault of the camera. Since the marking was on random pictures from the same roll, it wasn't a defective roll of film. And the pictures had been taken with different disposable cameras, over a two-year time period.

What was it? *Who* was it?

All we knew was that it was pretty interesting. I had never seen anything like it before. I have since learned that these markings are called "spirit orbs."

Two weeks passed, and two friends and I went to an author's lecture about staying connected to loved ones. It was interesting, but I was somewhat skeptical as I listened. I like my own stories, but have a difficult time believing the stories of others.

You were free to look around the book store after the lecture and discussion. If you purchased the author's book, he would autograph it for you and add a personal message.

My two friends and I separated and walked around the store on our own. After looking at several books, I picked up a copy of the book written by the speaker of the evening.

Leafing through it, I decided that there was nothing of interest in it for me. Since I wasn't going to purchase the book, I put it back down.

A soon as I set the book back down on the table, someone gave me a gentle shove in the middle of my back, a push toward the books and the table. I turned around to see who had pushed me. There was no one standing anywhere close to me.

Too weird. "Someone wants me to buy this book," I thought, although I had no idea who or why.

Picking up the book, I went over to the author and explained that I hadn't planned to purchase the book, but that "someone" had pushed me into it.

Telling him what had happened was a bit rude on my part. It was necessary, though, because my purchase was made due to extremely curious circumstances. I wanted him to know that strange detail. He was amused.

At home, I began looking through the book to try to figure out why I had been directed toward the purchase. Coming to the part about "recognizing spirit communications," I was drawn to a section about photographs.

It detailed how pictures are used to make contact, but that the contact often goes unnoticed. The suggestion was given to look at your photo albums, or other pictures, to see if you notice any unusual shadows, shapes or lights that you had not previously observed.

Remembering Maureen's pictures, I sat down and began to

look at pictures from my trips to Hawaii. These were pictures that had been taken using various disposable cameras, or my own camera, over several months, on different occasions, and in a variety of places.

I had looked at these pictures repeatedly, but had not before seen what I now saw. Not in every picture, and not located in the same place in the various pictures, there was an unusually-shaped, distinctive marking. It was one of the wildest things I had ever seen.

In each of these "special" pictures, there are two shapes: one somewhat hazy and the other in perfect focus. The shapes resembled what I call "stealth bombers," and each looks somewhat like a filled-in Peace sign.

Unusual images in pictures

It was outrageous, yet comforting at the same time. The images were also on the picture negatives. How could I have missed seeing this all of the countless other times that I had looked at the pictures?

I stayed up until 1:00 AM, looking at picture, after picture, after picture. I knew that I would be exhausted at school the next day, but I was fascinated, and I couldn't stop.

Having no idea who or what this shape could be, I showed the pictures to Kate and Moll.

Moll said, "I know who you think it is, but it's not."

Kate said nothing, but just looked. Later, trying to protect me from myself, she again cautioned me about sharing the pictures and their markings with too many people: "Not too many people will understand this, Mom."

The next day, after school, I spread the pictures out on a table, and asked Maureen if she noticed a commonality about them.

She replied, "Do I *notice* anything? This is unbelievable."

"Maureen, he's turned into a stealth bomber. But who's the other one traveling with him? This is too crazy."

I absolutely loved it, and so did Maureen.

She asked, "May I take these home to show my family?"

"Of course you may," I replied. "Let me know what they think."

Over time, I would look at pictures taken through the years, all taken when George was still alive. I was amazed to see these same shapes appearing in pictures taken over a wide expanse of time and place.

So, he hadn't turned into a stealth bomber after all ... We had been traveling with this contingent for years.

I had no idea what this phenomenon meant. I do know, however, that it was extremely interesting ...

RULE #2: The synchronicity of life events is astonishing!

It all had to happen in the proper sequence: Maureen showed me her pictures, I went to the lecture, bought the book, zeroed in on the part about photographs, and then took a good look at my pictures. Previously, I hadn't noticed the "communication" in the pictures. Now, it's the first thing that I look for when I have film developed.

And it took the synchronicity of these events to get my attention.

Check out your pictures; you may find some overlooked surprises!

The pendulum dowsing idea and the photography discovery took place within about two weeks of each other. I was delighted to be getting this information in quick turnover, rapid succession. It felt as if I were being thrown lifeline after lifeline after lifeline. I was extremely grateful for the happenings, but somewhat overwhelmed, too. I only knew one thing: "Thank you," to whomever, was in order.

The third type of connection I want to share with you has to do with energy.

If you have experienced this yourself, you know exactly what I am talking about. If you are unfamiliar with energy work, it is difficult and, perhaps, impossible for me to explain.

Since I am not certain as to how this works, I will simply say that I have grown to be able to handle it, to be amused by it, and to be warmed and comforted by its presence. I only know that energy connections are very real and reassuring to experience.

At first, after George died, I no longer wondered during the day where he was, or what he was doing, as I had when he was in his body.

That's because I knew right where he was, and exactly what he was doing. He was walking with me, on my right side, and, at times, holding my arm to support me. It was an amazingly strange sensation, welcomed and deeply appreciated.

In October 2002, nine months after George's death, the pendulum, the photographs and energy work all came together. I was also experiencing something else, but I didn't realize it at the time: soul travel.

For as long as I can remember, I have always felt that I solved problems when I slept. If something needed to be figured out, I always seemed to have the answer when I awoke the next morning.

But, now, after this "confluence of the three powers," not only could I solve problems, but I felt, upon awaking, as if I had been somewhere. I had no idea where I'd been, or what had taken place. I only knew—really knew—that I had traveled somewhere.

Never having read anything about this sort of thing, I didn't know that I was experiencing astral travel, soul travel. I still haven't done any reading or study in this area, but it is the next stage of learning that I am gong to explore.

In the meantime, I will just enjoy the feelings, the knowing that something has occurred, something quite out of this world.

That George and I are still connected has been explained to me in this way: water comes out of the faucet only when you turn it on; electrical power is in your home, but the lights don't go on until you flip the switch.

The power is always there. But we don't always use it. So, too, with connecting. The power for connection is always there.

Most often, though, we are unaware of how to "flip the switch." Those on the other side would dearly love for us to turn on all of the power, to make the connection, because the benefit to all of us is immense.

Do you know the feeling when someone is in the house with you, but they are taking a nap in another room? You know that they are there; you're just in different rooms ...

Carol said to think of it as if George were sleeping in another room. He's here; I just can't see him.

I understand and appreciate the concept, but my mind continues on with this thought: if someone were in my house, taking a nap, I could peek in the room to see them; not so with

George. I don't know where to peek. And, from this point, I can't see.
People have asked if I were ever angry at George for leaving. No, I can honestly say that I never conciously remember experiencing anger. How could I be angry at someone I had loved so much, and still loved? I just wanted him to wake up from his "nap" and come into the room where I could see him. But anger? No, I was never angry.

My reading has opened up my thinking not only to ideas about soul mates, but about soul families, as well. When my soul mate was standing where I could see, touch, and hear him, this was a concept that I had never thought about.

I knew we were pretty "together," but I didn't realize how "together" we had been.

I now know that we always have been and always will be, together, forever.

I feel extremely blessed to be part of a pretty terrific earth family and I am also beginning to realize that my soul family is no less great.

At last, I understand the final line in the Henry Van Dyke poem, "Time Is":

But for those who love,
Time is eternity.

I must have asked George the meaning of those lines a million times. Each time, he would patiently explain it to me. I'd forget and ask him again. I never have to ask any more, because I now know the exact meaning: it *is* forever.

Carol tells me that George and I have been connected for many lifetimes; that, at times after death, he waits for me and, at times, I wait for him.

Prior to this life, we agreed on this path. He agreed to "stick around" after his death.

I just want to know one thing: whatever made me agree to his leaving so early? I'd like to re-think that contract.

In a note to me, my friend, Kim Androw, wrote: "I've often thought that we are given so much extensive education to be lawyers, doctors, electricians, and teachers; but for life's most horrific and inevitable events, there is no training and very little guidance."

She is certainly correct. There was no point of reference in my life that prepared me for George's exit. Even if I thought I could have prepared, the preparation would have paled in comparison to the actual happening.

I'd like to say that I'm fine. And, really, I suppose that I *am* fine.

But it takes a while for traumatic mental and emotional pain to manifest itself in the physical:

- I've experienced an increase in blood pressure
- at times there is heightened anxiety because my "tag team" partner has disappeared
- I still have issues around cooking
- I have difficulty eating in the dining room where we ate our last meal
- my right leg feels as if I have a permanent charley horse.

Other than that, things have been manageable; manageable because, although I may look like I am alone, I am not.

I may appear to be alone, but I am never lonely; how could I be lonely? I am surrounded by an invisible support system that is beyond my limited earthly comprehension. Like rows of standing dominoes, everything in my life seems to line up and then fall into place when it is time to happen.

George loved the song by Cat Stevens: "You Only Dance On This Earth For A Short While."

I was privileged to have been his partner.

I still am ...
We still are partners.
My reason for writing these memoirs has evolved from my need to help myself, to a desire to help others. I am sharing my experiences with connecting in the hope that others will try them, connect with their loved ones, and be comforted.
My knowing—not just thinking, but knowing —that I am still connected to George, and will forever be connected, has made all the difference in the world to me. You are forever connected to those you have loved.
May it make all the difference in your world, too.

My extroverted side has allowed me to share these private ideas with you. Now my introverted side is taking over. To paraphrase Voltaire, in the very last line of my favorite book, *Candide*: "I feel that I must now cultivate [tend to] my own garden," and retreat for refuge into a Thoreau-like setting ...
... plus, Kate and Moll will not approve, nor appreciate, the fact that I have just revealed, publicly, what has been so very private.
I apologize to them.

PART FIVE:
AN ONGOING PRESENCE

ORDINARY MAN, EXTRAORDINARY SOUL

In life, George was a fount of information. His ability to remember facts and figures had earned him the nickname of "Stat Man" from some of Kate's friends. I'm not certain when or how he acquired his vast store of knowledge, but it was truly amazing.

Jeanine had always said that she and George should co-author a book titled *10,000 Useless Facts*. George could do the writing and, since Jeanine was a graduate of The Art Institute of Chicago, she could illustrate his work.

Almost from the moment of George's death, information and signs began appearing in swift succession.

At one point, I was getting overwhelmed and upset by the "things" that were happening.

Jeanine explained it this way: "You know how he gave rapid-fire information when he was here? Well, maybe now he's so excited about everything he's learning that he just wants to share it all with you, all at once. He's bombarding you with information. You could ask him to slow it down a little ... "

I loved the connections with George and, even though they could be somewhat intense, I never wanted them to stop. I told Jeanine that they could still write the book together. Now the title could be *10,000 Facts—From The Other Side ...*

Time after time, inexplicably beautiful things have happened. Depending on my mood, I would smile, cry, or laugh in response. But, always, I felt delightfully comforted.

George had accomplished so much in this lifetime. He had brought such joy into our lives and had been a help to so many. Now, he had infinitely multiplied his abilities to comfort, guide, assist, and laugh with us, from his new vantage point.

On an almost daily basis, I am compelled to say things such as:

"How did you do that, George?"

"I don't believe that just happened."
"That was pretty good, George."
"What was that all about?"
"Did you just see that?"

There wasn't a shortage of George stories before; there isn't a shortage of George stories now.

Throughout this narrative, I have related some curious happenings that I have attributed to George. Following are more experiences that have happened since his death.

I didn't notice, or at least I wasn't aware of, so many coincidences in my life before he died. Now, things are happening with incredible speed. Interesting experiences involving George have happened to others who have shared their stories with me, and they also have happened to me, with or without others being present.

For so many reasons, I wish that he were still here, here where I could see him; not only see him, but especially so that I could hear him explain how everything in this new dimension works.

I have no idea how he has managed to do the following deeds, but, explanations from him or not, I hope it all continues. Some pretty amazing, out-of-this-world feats have indeed transpired.

George was an ordinary, but definitely unique, human being. He is now an extraordinary, and definitely unique, soul!

And so, the saga of George Portenlanger continues, with a listing of my favorite, fascinating incidents that keep us linked together in unusual and unexpected ways.

Georgie, I know the "why," it's the "how" I don't understand. Others have been used to channel your thoughts and actions into our earthly lives. You have moved people into place, and given them inspiration, in order to help us. I hope you know that we are grateful and thankful for the times in which you have been instrumental in these unexpected happenings:

∞   Two weeks after gluttons ate my special pie, right before bedtime, I received the gift of another huge, delicious banana cream pie from an unexpected, but connected, source. I know you were the one who prompted the "return."

∞ When I walked into the historic Mokuaikaua Church in Kailua-Kona and sat down to meditate alone in the beautiful surroundings, a woman walked out from behind the altar. She went to the piano at the front of the sanctuary, sat down, and played "You'll Never Walk Alone," finished and, silently, left. What a powerful message.

∞ In need of a sign, I asked you to send something. Going into the TV room, I randomly selected a tape to put into the VCR. It was the one where you and Margaret were on a trip out East and I was back at home. The tape began at the place where you were eating. Looking right into the camera you say: "Hi, Betty; wish you were here!" I looked at the TV and said: "Hi, George. I wish *you* were here." I replayed that over and over and over.

∞ Who is that guy with the dog? I never saw him before in the 30-plus years we've lived here. Now, all of a sudden, he starts showing up, unexpectedly, at key moments and times, such as on my birthday or on your birthday when I'm extremely sad. It's curious that he resembles you in age, size and manner of dress. Plus, he walks a "Max"-type dog. Keep sending him.

∞ When Carol said that you wanted me to go to Oktoberfest, I went and couldn't figure out why you wanted that. It was jammed wall-to-wall with people. Mary and I were about to leave; we had almost turned the corner when Chris, the paramedic who tried so desperately to save you, called my name. In that incredibly crowded place, I was able to introduce her to Mary: "Mary, this is the wonderful angel who appeared and helped your brother and me last January." You gave Mary a beautiful gift that evening, and she and I realized, at once, why you had wanted us to go.

∞ I remember the incident when the dog ran in front of Margaret's car on the slick, snow-covered, busy street, two weeks after you died. Poor Moll, lover of animals that she is, hit and killed the huge dog. It was a totally wretched experience! The next day, she was following a car that had a bumper sticker that read: "My karma ran over my dogma." Thank you for the comic relief, sent in true George fashion.

∞ When your brother, John, was at school, talking about you to a fellow teacher, they were alone, when the computer printer at the opposite end of the room began to print something. The two of them walked across the room and looked on in amazement as the printer printed out a single sheet of paper, empty except for a tiny heart graphic in the top, left-hand corner. John said: "I know there has to be some rational explanation for this, but I don't want to hear it."

♥

∞ Waiting to board the plane for Hawaii, I was the last passenger left at the gate. The attendant, speaking over the PA system, said: "Will passenger Duckworth please approach the counter." There was absolutely no one anywhere in sight close to the gate. I was completely alone. "Duckworth" was the name you had given the man with the odd running style who jogged with you at the park. I spoke inside my mind, saying: "Let's go George!" We then got on the plane.

∞ At Old World Wisconsin, when several of us went for a day trip, a butterfly rode on your brother, Joe's, shirt collar. It was unbelievable that it stayed on his shirt for about 45 minutes. When we arrived at the German farm, it flew off, as if it had reached home.

∞ When I was alone, and so ill, during one trip to Hawaii, upon waking up in the morning, I heard a voice in my head say, "Betty, go to the doctor!" Looking in the phone book, I opened to the "Physicians" page and the first address I saw was for a walk-in clinic a block from my hotel. Precise timing and location saved me from a serious infection.

∞ Kate had trained for the Chicago Marathon. The two of you had discussed her participation and she was looking forward to the race with her whole heart and soul. It was a commitment, not only to herself, but now had become a commitment to you, as well. A week before the event, knee pain put the idea of her running the race in doubt. A visit to the doctor allayed fears of any permanent problem. It was determined that she would, indeed, be able to be part of this exciting event. Upon leaving the doctor's office to return to work, she was blocked at the crosswalk of that busy downtown intersection by a city bus. The ad on the side of the bus that was stopped right in front of her face read: "I'm running the last mile with my Dad." That day she had received the go-ahead, not only from her doctor, but her father, too. She did, indeed, run with her Dad. The two of you had a great race, and Kate finished the 26.2 miles in 4 ½ hours. Great timing on that ad.

∞ Parking spaces appear out of nowhere. I am so grateful. Just ask and it happens.

∞ George was an electrician who loved squirrels. He felt that they were quite industrious, and he always marveled that he'd never seen a lazy squirrel. That's why it was so curious when the squirrels chewed through the electrical wires at school and shut off the power for the day. That was a new experience, and one for which everyone credited George. They loved him for getting us some time off!

∞ Was that automatic writing, when the two little smiley faces appeared in my journal? Exactly how did that happen? I'd love to know that answer. Really, I'd love to know ...

∞ Then there was the *Power of Now* book that I loaned to a totally unreliable friend. Realizing that he would never return it, I was resigned to the fact that I would never see it again. Much to my delight and surprise, I then received the book as a gift from one of my students. The amazing part was that the child who gave me the book reminded me of the brother of the person to whom I had given *my* copy of the book. So, not only did I get the book "back," but the vehicle who gave it back to me reminded me of the "keeper's" sibling, as though he were making up for his brother's lapse.

∞ Margaret and I were discussing a social issue of a personal nature. I was wishing that you were around, in order for you to lend your advice. It was getting quite serious, and we continued to talk as I walked up the stairs and into my bedroom. As I stood there, next to the side of the bed that you had slept on, the light bulb in the lamp on the bedside table exploded. It just shattered, for no apparent reason. The light hadn't even been turned on. In all of my 57 years, I had never seen anything like it! Shards of glass were everywhere! I guess that you, the electrician, had been part of the discussion after all. It took us a while to clean up your answer to her question. We worked in silence and the issue was never again discussed.

∞ Then there was the time in school when I was talking with a child, and my hand began to itch. I looked down to see what was on it. There, on the top of my hand, was a capital letter G, inside a circle. It was as if I had been branded.
Showing it to Jeanine, I asked: "What is this?"
She said: "It's a circle with the letter G inside."
"Why is it on my hand?" I asked.
Running upstairs to Maureen's room, I asked her the same question. She gave the same response as Jeanine had given.
By the time I had returned to my room, the "G" was beginning to fade. There was no logical explanation for the marking, and I was completely unnerved. The next day, crying, I told Jeanine and Maureen that I thought I was losing my mind. They assured me that they had seen it, too, and that they weren't losing *their* minds. It had really happened; they verified it. Even so, it was still totally unsettling!

∞ One other time, the circle and G reappeared. I was driving my mother home from the hospital. As we left the parking lot, I glanced at my hand on the steering wheel and I noticed the marking again. I showed my hand to my mother and she confirmed what I saw. She, however, seemed to think that it was a perfectly normal occurrence. Though it seemed anything but normal to me, I took its presence to mean that you were there with me, George, helping me— a very comforting sign.

∞ One of the wildest incidents that has happened involved what I call "the catapulting tree." I was hosting a Christmas luncheon. The first two guests had arrived and we were in the dining room, talking about Christmas cards. I had just remarked that I hadn't sent any cards that year. In the past, I had made the whole family each contribute a personal message on the card. George was usually the last to write, and always had ended with: "They've said it all. Merry Christmas. Love, George." No sooner had I finished that sentence than a little tree, decorated with my "teacher" ornaments and sitting on a sideboard on the other side of the room, levitated, then catapulted off the sideboard and crashed to the floor. The three of us stood there, looking at the smashed tree. For a moment, we were stunned into silence. It was something that was beyond description, and I was filled with gratitude that two other people had been there with me to witness the incident, to verify that it had actually happened.

ORCHESTRATING BETH AND BETTY

I *must say, George, that one of your most involved maneuvers occurred in San Diego. I'll never get over this experience!*

I called Carol Dirck in March of 2003, and said that I was going to Hawaii that summer, in July. If possible, I would like to meet her in person. I had been so comforted during our phone conversations that I wanted to see her face-to-face.

On my way to Hawaii, I suggested that, if Carol was going to be at home, I could stop in Southern California for a day or two. I would be meeting Joan and Lois there anyway because the three of us would be continuing on to Hawaii.

Carol said, "I see a fourth person with you."

I replied, "It's you, Carol; you're the fourth person."

"No, it's not me; it's someone else who is with you."

"No, just the three of us will be there." I said.

We left it at that.

Beth, a friend in Chicago, had heard me talk about Carol. Since she seemed interested, I gave her Carol's card. Time evaporated, a year went by, and Beth had never had the chance to call and connect with Carol.

Beth and I teach together and, in June, we said good-bye for the summer vacation. I was excited about returning to Hawaii the next month, but didn't know what Beth had planned for her time off.

Flying from San Francisco to San Jose, I was to meet Carol for the first time. She picked me up at the airport, and I was delighted to see, finally, "my bridge" in person.

We decided, on the spur of the moment, to go to Old Town in San Diego. After looking at the marvelous shops, lunch was in order. Sitting in the open courtyard, we had a delightful and unusual meeting. Not only was the food delicious but the air was electric, and supercharged with energy.

The ensuing conversation was to be beyond belief.

Halfway through the meal, Carol said that George was

insisting that we leave and go to a specific open air shop. I said, "Tell him that he will have to wait, because I'm not finished with my meal. Or, I guess that I can tell him myself."

Out loud, to the air, I said: "You'll have to wait, George." I continued to eat.

Carol said, "He is really getting quite forceful and insists that we go, *now!*" Reluctantly, I agreed to leave.

As we walked along, I was taking my time looking into shops and Carol kept saying, "He's getting almost rude, and he wants us to hurry up!"

I kept saying, "This is so silly. What are we doing? How do you know what he's saying?"

All the while, Carol was also trying to understand just why we were being directed to this one specific shop: *walk over one block; go down two blocks; turn and continue walking 1 ½ blocks.*

When we reached our destination, I couldn't understand it, either.

Stepping inside the gated open market area, filled with wind chimes and huge clay and ceramic pottery, I said out loud, "George, what am I supposed to buy here? It won't fit into my suitcase!"

As soon as the words were out of my mouth, I felt a tap, tap, tap on my shoulder. Was I afraid to turn around?

You know I was.

But I did turn around—and there stood Beth.

All I could say was, "Beth!"

All she could say was, "Betty!"

When we finally stopped saying, "Beth!" "Betty!" "Beth!" "Betty!" I managed to say, "Beth, this is Carol Dirck. Carol, this is my friend, Beth."

It had taken over a year and a few thousand miles, but Beth was finally talking with Carol.

Along with Beth was her future husband, Ron. Beth and I talked about the amazing set of circumstances that had ended in our meeting.

I'm not certain what Ron and Carol talked about; I just know that Beth and I kept doing the "Beth!" "Betty!" routine.

We all stood there for 45 minutes, talking and laughing, and thrilled with the unseen power that had been used to guide four people to the same place at the same time.

Just a minute one way or the other, and we would have missed the connection.

It even turned out that Beth had forgotten some cards that she had purchased and had returned to the store to pick them up. Now we understood why she had to forget them. In order for all this to work out perfectly, she had to double back, because I was taking too long eating my lunch.

(It was my fault, entirely. No wonder he was getting so insistent!)

After George had worked to orchestrate the activity of four people—Beth, Ron, Carol and me—I had almost blown it for dear George. All his powerful energy hung in the balance of my slow pace ...

We decided that, since this had been such a phenomenal meeting, we simply had to purchase something at the shop. We had to, because George had worked so hard to bring us all together. And, not only had he worked so hard, but he had worked so very *long.*

This was July, and he had started way back in March, when I had spoken with Carol, and she had said that there was a fourth person she saw in California with me. "No, just three: Joan, Lois and me," I had insisted. Little did I know that Beth was to be the fourth!

That was pretty good, George. How did you ever manage to pull it off?

What a wild, wild, wild, wonderfully wild and powerful experience. I felt at once both exhausted and exalted; exhausted, exalted and confounded.

Really, George. How does this all work?
I love you!

21 JUST A FEW MORE STORIES, I PROMISE!

I could go on at endless length about all of the "George" things that have happened since his death.
But please permit me just a few more:

∞ Many times, when Jeanine and I talk by phone, something odd happens.
During one phone conversation, an old-fashioned phone began to ring inside our phones, and faint, strange voices began speaking. Frightened, but laughing, we hang up immediately. Instead of hanging up, we should have said, "Hi, George!" and kept on talking.

∞ There are times at school when the children get too noisy and I turn off the lights to get their attention and quiet them down. One day, when I was a bit short-tempered, the lights went off in the room, as if to get my attention and quiet *me* down. It certainly did work, and it got me back on track, instantly.

∞ A boost from George happened when meeting John in the crowded Paulina Market at Christmas time. A lady gave us her #44 ticket so that we could move up in line. The best part was that #44 was an inside joke of George's that John and I both knew.

∞ Then, there have been all of the people named "George" that I have met in Hawaii, including the gardener named "Keoki." You guessed it; that's "George" in Hawaiian.

∞ A confirming connection was made that involved my bracelet, the last Christmas present I had received from George. I lost

Just a few More Stories, I Promise!

it in San Francisco and then "found" it in an unbelievably private way ...

∞ Another bracelet event happened the summer after George died, on the date of our wedding anniversary.

I was at an art fair with my good friend, Kathi. In one of the jewelry booths, I saw a beautiful pearl bracelet with a silver heart locket. It was perfectly priced, and I knew that, if George had been standing next to me, he would have said, "Do you like it? Get it, Betty."

I also knew that I had enough jewelry to last several lifetimes and that I didn't need another piece.

After walking around and looking at the bracelet from every angle, I decided not to make the purchase. As I turned to leave, one of the owners walked back into the booth. She said to her friend, "I was just at the food tent and saw George. He says 'Hi'."

I thought of the George that I knew. *He* would be at the food tent; how nice of him to say "Hello."

That sealed the deal; I purchased the bracelet. As the woman was wrapping up my item, I explained to her why I had decided to make the purchase.

Upon my finishing the story, she said, "There are no consequences." Too funny; of course, she meant "there are no *coincidences.*"

There aren't. Everything is planned; planned more perfectly than we could ever imagine, and more sequentially than we could ever dream.

George, the help you have sent has been received with thankful gratitude.

The humor you have sent, along with the help, has been more than a delight.

129

We wouldn't have expected anything less. It is a continuation of your earthly personality, and it is precious!

I'm thrilled that you are still with us, but if you were going to hang around ... why didn't you just stay in your body?

Talking to candles just doesn't seem to cut it.

I miss you. I miss the human, the physical, you.

SOME DREAMS

Only once do I remember a dream where George was so funny that I actually woke up laughing out loud.

I am not conscious of the many other actual dreams that I've had about George, but I am certain that they are numerous.

Often when I wake up, I feel as if I have been somewhere. During the night, I feel that I have not just been in a dream state, but awake, and at such times I have the feeling, and an actual, real knowing, that I have been somewhere.

Upon waking, I am once again confined to earthly parameters, and have no recollection of where I've traveled or what has taken place.

I have had three visitations. *Visitations* are different from dreams or manifestations. I explain them this way: in a "visitation," all of your senses are involved; the colors are vivid; the person is there; and you are in a dreamlike state.

In the first visitation, George directed a very personal message to me. For days I had been replaying, in my brain, all of the times during our life together when I had wasted time complaining about trivial, unimportant "stuff."

I was punishing myself with the fact that I had wasted precious time; I couldn't rewind my life and get those minutes and hours back. The thought of this would not go away; I was obsessing over something I couldn't change. Why had I been so foolish to waste our limited time together?

One night, appearing to be standing right there, George said, "Forget the lost time."

"I shouldn't worry, then?" I responded.

Our eyes locked, he shook his head "no" and then slowly withdrew, as I said, "OK." Relieved, I kept thinking of the words he had used.

He had referred to "the lost time." He hadn't said "the wasted time." To me, that made a huge difference. It was so powerful that

I was released from the recurring thought that had been causing me such deep anguish.

The two other visitations carried intensely meaningful messages, as well. One showed me that George was physically all right and the other let me know that he will continually be there to help me.

They were dynamic, electrifying, beautiful and comforting.

I love it when friends share their George dreams with me; I love the messages. Most of the time, they're right on target. At other times, I have no idea as to their meaning.

Lois' e-mails regarding two dreams that she had had about George are very special to me. How kind of him to let her know how much she means to all of us.

From Lois

To Betty

Tuesday, September 16, 2003, 8:09 PM

George came to me in a dream last night and gave me a HUGE hug.... I was telling him about how much fun we were having. It was an amazing experience. I woke feeling very hugged. Thank you, George. I guess it was his way of saying thanks. Not a dream / it was real. xo, L

From Betty

To Lois

Tuesday, September 16, 2003, 101:42 PM

LOIS, I LOVE YOUR DREAM!

Did he really do that? THANK YOU for telling me. And, thank you Geo for letting Lois know how wonderful she is. Last night, I was doing what Carol taught me to do —— trying to "see" him. (The only time that I have really seen him was in the hotel room on Oahu and it was a tornado-like thing—did I ever tell you about that? It was out of this world.) I just never seem to have the time to center down and try to connect. Don't know if I just thought it was working, but it really was an interesting experience. I think I was able to do it—at least a little bit. On second thought, I didn't really do anything. Maybe he was hanging around the earth's atmosphere, waiting to let you know that he appreciates EVERYTHING that you have done for us ... beginning with introducing me to Carol and ALL of the other incredible, unbelievable, innumerable experiences. PLUS, he always talked about what a great cook you were/are. Maybe he also wanted to thank you for that fabulous egg dish we had when we visited you in SF whatever year that was. He loved it. I love it that he was in your dream. *GO GEORGIE. GO GEORGIE. GO GEORGIE.*

You made my day/night with your dream report. Thank you. xo, Betty

From Lois

To Betty

Tuesday, September 16, 2003, 10:51 PM

Oh good. Incidentally, he looked rather fit.

L

From Betty

To Lois

Tuesday, September 16, 2003, 11:25 PM

That is too funny. Way to go George. He must be exercising. I am thrilled with your George reports.

xo

From Lois

To Betty

Wednesday, September 17, 2003, 5:55AM

Yep, even more fit than Arnold. He was in a suit!

L

From Lois

To Betty

Sunday, January 4, 2004, 12:27 PM

Ok, here's one for your "George book." Yesterday, I noticed that the dimmer for the switch for the light that washes the wall just as you enter our bedroom was broken. Wouldn't dim at all. Would only stay on HIGH no matter where the slide was positioned.

I went to bed and a HUGE storm came up around 4am. Tremendous rain and wind—very monsoon like in its energy and excitement. I stayed awake to watch and listen, closed the doors in the house and tried getting back to sleep. No success.

I was thinking about George and began a conversation thanking him for taking such good care of you, knowing how much the two of you still loved each other, etc. I rolled over and THE LIGHT WAS ON .... Not the light at full intensity as earlier in the day, but only a soft, dimmed light. I walked over to the switch, turned it off and said, "Ok, George, that was great! Do it again." He didn't. But this morning when I turned the light on, there was no dimming capacity—impossible to recreate last night's level. Oh boy, George, thank you for stopping by. xo, L

I love her e-mail, and I love it that George shares his energy with others.

Then there was Sue's dream, where George was walking down the street toward our house with his suitcase. Once inside the house, he appeared on the TV screen, and little shards of light, shaped in unusual electrical symbols, filled the atmosphere.

I thank her for each happening that she has documented. May the dreams keep coming and the connections never end.

Kate and Moll have been the fortunate recipients of vivid dreams and manifestations.

One night, George called Kate on the phone. When she asked him how he was, and what he was doing, he said that he "was fine and out traveling around." When she woke up, she was sitting on her bed, with the phone in her hand, listening to the dial tone.

Margaret woke up quite early one morning to see him standing in her room, looking at her, wearing his favorite sleeveless T-shirt and his "I love you Dad" boxer shorts. He said nothing, bent over to pick something up off the floor, stood back up, and folded his arms across his chest. She was so unnerved that she closed her eyes and pulled the covers up over her head. I told her that she should have spoken to him and told him that she was thrilled to see him, but that he was frightening her, and ask him what he wanted ...

... as if I would have been able to speak out loud if I had been in her place! I'd love to have the chance to find out exactly what I would do in that situation; probably start screaming, yelling, and running around the house, scaring the wits out of him.

No wonder I've never had a manifestation from him. He never could tolerate loud noises.

SHARING GEORGE

I absolutely love it that people still feel connected to George. It confirms my perception of connection and helps me feel that I am not totally deluded or crazed.

What fun, to get notes that read "George told me to buy this for you." Or to have people say, "What's George been up to lately? Tell him I say 'Hi'." Or "Could you please ask George what he thinks about …"

The best was one time when I was in Margaret's room. I can't remember what the conversation was about, but she said, "Would the two of you please get out of my room?"

She was serious, and I loved it.

How interesting was it the other day, when Kate said to Margaret, "Ask him, Moll. He's right about 75% of the time."

How funny was that? Kate and Moll are being converted, and they don't even realize it.

Maybe they do realize it. They are becoming reluctant, but grateful, converts, compliments of their father.

So many people have said that they ask George for help with various aspects of their lives. How cute is that?

I certainly don't mind sharing him, but sometimes I must admit that I think, "Get your own George." Like the song says: he's "takin' care of business and working overtime." Taking care of business for his dear family and putting in some serious overtime for everybody else. Heavy-duty, serious overtime for all of us.

He did it on earth. Poor guy.

He's doing it in the spirit world. Poor soul.

Actually, there's nothing "poor" about his soul. He is remarkable and we are in awe. It is a privilege to share our wonderful George.

24 DECODING THE GIFT

Just as children coming into my kindergarten class need help with decoding and sounding out words on their journey toward learning to read, I, too, needed, and continue to need, help in decoding the signs in my life.

The information is there but, most of the time, I'm still at the "pre-reading" stage.

I am working on it. But I am, at times, a very slow learner.

George's messages have been powerful. They are received with delight and gratitude. It is my hope that they will continue until I take my last breath.

Actually, I know that they will continue, but not because I am clingy, weak or desperate. They will continue because we are connected on a soul level and he has agreed to help me for this entire lifetime.

He is my Anam Cara, and I am delighted by that fact. I only hope that he knows how much I value his love and friendship. I'm certain that he does.

I also hope that I am his soul friend, in return. That would be an honor for me, an honor I would not take lightly. It would be one of my greatest accomplishments.

I believe that we are all connected to a higher power. Because of the religious teaching I've received in my life, I call that higher power God; others may use another name.

If, as I believe, we are made in the likeness and image of God/The Higher Power, then we are all a part of God, and God is a part of all of us. Therefore, when I say that "George" is sending tremendous help, I suppose I mean that God is sending the help. George is receiving the "power" directly from "The Source" and relaying the bounty on to us.

In my limited understanding, there is only one thing of which I am certain: I am connected. It is with thanksgiving in my heart and mind that I keep the connections open so that the energy will continue to flow.

I need all the help I can get in this lifetime.
I am not greedy; I am grateful.

To all of us who knew him, George was a gift that we were given. His scope and magnitude continue to enrich and bless our lives.

As Elizabeth Barrett Browning wrote in "Sonnets from the Portuguese":

How do I love thee? Let me count the ways.
....
With my lost Saints—I love thee with the breath,
Smiles, tears, of all my life!—and, if God choose,
I shall but love thee better after death.

PART SIX: ACCEPTING THE PROCESS

UNCHARTED WATERS

Was it in the plan for George to leave so that I could learn? Perhaps.

Since George's death, my thinking on many issues has changed and evolved. The area of greatest change has come about with regard to my thoughts on the afterlife.

If I had thought about that subject at all prior to his death, it was never with the intense scrutiny with which I thought about it afterwards.

In my limited, earthly way, I feel myself growing and changing; hopefully, growing and changing in an upward and positive direction.

My mind has been newly opened to numerous possibilities and ideas. I have learned about energy, and how there are those who give you energy and there are those who take your energy. I have learned that there is

- negative energy
- positive energy
- rejuvenating energy
- emotional energy
- energy vibrations, and
- the energy of abundance: spiritual energy.

I have learned about energy vampires, spiritual cavemen, and the misuse of time—time, our most important non-renewable resource. I have learned about the sequencing of events, predestination, free will, soul mates and soul families.

I have learned to "go within, or go without." I have learned that whatever I need is provided at precisely the right moment. Green light, green light, green light. It is a delight to watch my life unfold with perfect timing.

Some people, along the way, felt that I wasn't grieving properly, although I have no idea what "grieving properly" means. I am definitely sure that there is more than just one "proper" way to get through grief.

If I cried, I was told that maybe I should go to therapy. If I didn't cry, it was suggested that maybe I wasn't allowing myself to mourn.

It reached the point where I found all of the advice to be somewhat humorous, although, sometimes, I became angry. And on days when my energy level was down, unwanted advice would dissolve me into tears, like waves washing over me. There was nothing I could do but ride it out.

I told Kate and Moll: whatever way you choose to get through this will be the right way. Do or don't do whatever you wish. We are in uncharted waters.

As my dear mother-in-law, Cora, was fond of saying, "No one dies conveniently anymore." We would laugh, and say: "What could that possibly mean?"

Well, I now understand and, Cora, you can say that again!

George, this wasn't convenient. You are fortunate that you won't be around to experience your years of sweet decay.

"Sweet decay" was the name he had given to old age.

But, weren't we supposed to go on a cruise across the Atlantic when I quit work next year? How inconvenient of you to bail early.

When George died, my life was devastated. Every room in the beautiful new home that we had built together reflected that devastation. His absence permeated the living room, the dining room, the kitchen, the TV room, the bedroom, the bathroom, and even the garden.

The crater-sized void left by his disappearance stretched as far and wide as my eyes could see and my heart could feel. The silence was deafening. As if I were a small child, I wanted to throw a tantrum and scream.

I liked my life the way it used to be. I didn't want to be forced into change. I didn't want to re-learn how to live. I was cut adrift, and I didn't like it.

I have always felt as if I were the wealthiest woman on the face of this earth. When Kate and Moll were young and I would say that, they would wonder aloud, "If you're so wealthy, why is our car rusty and falling apart?" I would just smile. I knew real wealth, and it had nothing to do with money.

Well ... I still feel that I am the wealthiest woman on the face of this earth. I have been given blessings and abundance on so many levels.

I can't remember where I read about the following idea, but think about it—it makes complete sense:

You want to give someone the perfect gift. You thoughtfully consider what they might like, plan the shopping trip and put forth great effort and energy into getting the exact item that they need or will delight in receiving.

After accepting the gift, they never express any gratitude, acknowledgement, or thanks.

The next time they are celebrating a special occasion, how much time do you think you will spend on choosing just the right gift for them?

So, too, with the Universe. It delights in giving us perfect gifts. Yet, how many times do we leave the gifts unopened, don't even see them, or, if we do recognize the gifts, simply forget to say, "Thank you!"

In my life, my God, the heavens, the universe, George, my spirit guides, Mark and Sheila—all of the above (choose the name with which you are most comfortable that encompasses them all)—have, from the moment of my birth, sent showers of remarkable blessings into my life. I have also experienced some rather *unusual* happenings in this lifetime, both positive and negative.

From each experience, even the horrendously negative ones, the outcome has always been positive. I feel that I have led a charmed life, and that I can truly say that I love the rhythm with which this life of mine flows.

We are not meant to live from the standpoint of scarcity. Rather, we are meant to gratefully live from the vantage point of abundance. So, try it. Delight in the abundant gifts that come your way. You will be amazed at what you receive, and you will not be disappointed. But, remember, never forget to say "Thank you!"

George loved a small book, *Buddha's Little Instruction Book*, by Jack Kornfield. It is a book of simple sayings with complex meanings:
"We are not independent, but interdependent."
"The trouble is, you think you have time."
"When asked, 'Are you a God or a man?', the Buddha replied, 'I am awake'."
"When you walk, just walk; when you eat, just eat."
"All things are like a river. We never step in the same river twice."

His favorite saying from the book was: "Live every act fully, as if it were your last."

George's last act on this earth was asking for help for me as we were about to be involved in the accident. Even though he was dying, his thoughts were not for himself.

How unselfish. He gave me such a beautiful gift at the very moment he was leaving. There is not enough money on earth to buy that love. What a legacy he left for us all: unselfish kindness and love. Nothing else matters. Nothing.

So often on our walks around the park, I would say, "George, do you think that everyone is as happy as we are?"

"No, Betty, I don't."
"Yes, I think they are."
"No, Betty, you just want them to be."
At the time, I didn't fully realize my unique situation. I now do.
Thank you, George, for the incredible happiness we shared. I was truly blessed and I continue to be so. I know I will never be separated from that love. But it's the physical separation that makes the ache so tremendous.
Please come back, Georgie, if only for a moment.

At times I visualize my life as if I am floating in a huge, black inner tube along a narrow, winding, meandering river: floating lazily along, then encountering rapids, getting pitched about, smashing on the bank, reaching smooth water, and then floating on.

This happens over and over, and one never knows what will be around the next bend and when the next set of rapids will appear. I know that I signed up for this particular river ride, but I forgot the reason why at the moment of my birth.

All I know is that I wonder who I really am and how I am connected to the people I encounter on this journey called my life. I am learning some interesting lessons.

If there are indeed seasons of the heart, my heart went into Winter and hibernation in January, 2002. It is now January, 2004, and, while I feel I am still in Winter, there are noticeable changes that point to the coming of Spring. It's not quite Spring, but its signs are starting to appear.

The first year, I was preoccupied with paperwork. The second year, in retrospect, was more difficult than the first. I didn't really realize it until after the second Christmas and the emotional exhaustion that followed the holiday. A changing in my attitude, a letting-go of traditions, an "OK, I don't really have to keep doing that anymore" realization—all took a toll.

I then did something that I had never done before in my life: I went to bed for two days.

The third year now looms ahead. I will continue my life, but what will be the who, what, how, where, when, and why of it? It will all unfold.

Carol Dirck calls change "growth," a positive experience. While I try to stay positively focused, as to the outcome of *this* change, at times I find it sad and wearisome.

Simply put, I miss him. I have had what some would call my share of life's "growth experiences." I have learned, over time, that change is not a bad thing. However, undergoing change requires effort and, at times, that effort can be tiring.

Change equals growth. I know that I have grown since George's death.

I will just have to wait to see where my life takes me now because of that Change; that unexpected, unwelcomed, uncharted Change ...

Postscript:
Since my mind has a way of forgetting, I wrote this story. I wrote it for me, so that I will always remember. I find him too beautiful to forget.

PART SEVEN: ADDENDA

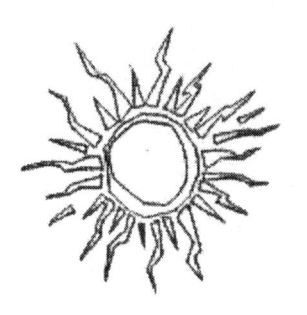

ADDENDA

RANDOM THOUGHTS AND NOTES

This book was written, from 2002 to 2004, in:
- Key West, Florida
- Captain Cook, The Big Island, Hawaii
- Kona, The Big Island, Hawaii
- Kapulena/Honokaa, The Big Island, Hawaii
- Chicago, Illinois

Things I did to survive:
- Traveled
- Bought shoes
- Learned to drink wine
- Blasted CDs on the stereo
- Became the e-mail queen
- Swore for the first three months
- Scheduled and received numerous massages

Books read during these two years:
(in random order)
1. *Soul Mates,* by Richard Webster
2. *Anam Cara,* by John O'Donohue
3. *7 Paths To God,* by Joan Borysenko, PhD.
4. *Journey Of Souls,* by Michael Newton
5. *Destiny Of Souls,* by Michael Newton
6. *One Last Time,* by John Edward
7. *The Lovely Bones,* by Alice Sebold
8. *The Power Of Now,* by Eckhart Tolle
9. *Your Seven Energy Centers,* by Elizabeth Clare Prophet and Patricia R. Spadaro
10. *Reaching Heaven,* by James Van Praagh
11. *Heaven And Earth,* by James Van Praagh
12. *Talking To Heaven,* by James Van Praagh

13. *The Tibetan Book Of Living And Dying,* by Sogyal Rinoche
14. *Wheels Of Light,* by Rosalyn L. Bruyere
15. *In Lieu Of Flowers,* by Nancy Cobb
16. *Death Of A Husband,* by Helen Reichert Lamben
17. *The Light In The Living Room,* by Gates McKibbin, PhD.
18. *Loveline,* by Gates McKibbin, PhD.
19. *A Course In Courage,* by Gates McKibbin, PhD.
20. *A Handbook On Hope,* by Gates McKibbin, PhD.
21. *The Life Of The Soul,* by Gates McKibbin, PhD.
22. *Available Wisdom,* by Gates McKibbin, PhD.
23. *Life After Loss,* by Raymond A. Moody Jr. and Dianne Arcangel
24. *Messages From The Masters,* by Brian L. Weiss, M.D.
25. *Many Lives, Many Masters,* by Brian L. Weiss, M.D.
26. *A Grief Observed,* by C.S. Lewis
27. *Never Say Goodbye,* by Patrick Matthews
28. *I Heard God Laughing: Renderings Of Hafiz,* by Daniel Ladinsky
29. *Illuminated Prayers,* by Marianne Williamson

Two final comments:
The quickness of death prevented me from ever telling George something that I had thought about, but never verbalized, over the years. I still feel disturbed about the Hawaiian glass, from McDonald's, back in the early 80's. He knows what I mean. Therefore, I am publicly apologizing. Why did I make such a big deal about bringing it home in the suitcase? I am so sorry.

And,

I know that I did not write this book on my own. Thank you for writing it with me.

AFTERWORD

I would love to hear from you, my reader, about what sort of response you may have felt from this book. Questions or comments? Your messages are always welcome. If a reply is required, please include a self-addressed, stamped envelope.

Betty Portenlanger
P.O. Box 31244
Chicago, Illinois 60631
E-mail: travelgeorge1@aol.com

I will post resources and various news items that might interest you on this blog site:

http://thankyouisinorder.blogspot.com

Additional copies of this book may be ordered 24/7, direct from Trafford Publishers, at their site, www.trafford.com, or by calling their toll-free number, 1-888-232-4444 (ask for "order desk").

I appreciate your interest in what I have had to share.
With Love, Betty

Betty, on Achill Island, Ireland

"One of the many places that I've visited while 'traveling with George.'"

APPENDIX:
E-MAILING HEAVEN

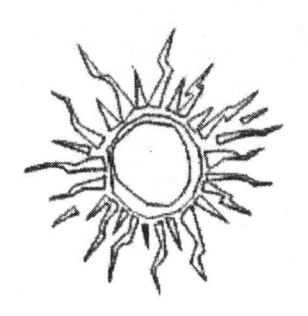

E-MAILING HEAVEN

This section, at the end of the book contains e-mails that I wrote over the time frame of a year-and-a-half.

In most of it, I am writing to George. At the time, I never intended for the writing to become public. However, I have decided to include the messages as part of my story because I realized that they are a journal of my personal attempt to survive.

Had I not written down my feelings, I would never have remembered them. Now, as I re-read the messages, many of the thoughts expressed seem foreign to me—and unbelievably redundant—as if written by another.

If you have ever been in a situation similar to the one I was experiencing, you will understand the place of desperation and anguish from which I was writing. From the vantage point of where I now stand, the reoccurrence of words is quite evident. I was repeating certain phrases over and over and over, as if I could not move on. At that point, I *couldn't* move on. I was just trying to survive from day to day. That very repetition is the reason I was able to endure.

The words are sincere and they came from the very depths of my being. Over time, the messages evolved. Hopefully, so did I.

In some places where I was writing privately to George, there may be, perhaps, some things that will be confusing to you. I apologize; that was not my intention in including them. I simply feel that the writing in its totality does have "reality" value, and I, therefore, would like to share the messages with you. In order not to interrupt the flow of my narrative, I decided to put the e-mails at the end of the book, where you now find them.

But first, here is a different kind of interchange, one that shows the process of grief and acceptance that was going on in my family.

From Kate

To me

Subj: I just...

Date: Tuesday, September 26, 2002 10:02 AM

...wanted to drop a little email to let you know that I love you. I was thinking yesterday and the day before all about Dad and that whole fiasco at the hospital. It wouldn't stop replaying and replaying and replaying... drives me nuts sometimes. But then all I have to do is just think of him saying HOOOOOOLLLD IT! Or telling me how unbelievable I am for watching such junk on TV and it makes me laugh.

Or just picture him in that stupid hat with Molly interviewing him on the ship...what a riot! Thank the Lord for that damn camera that I thought I hated and now it is priceless.

Anyway, I truly admire you and how you are coping with it all... you're amazing.

Love, Katie

From me

To Kate

Subj: Re: I just...

Date: Tuesday, September 26, 2002 3:43 PM

Dear Kate,

Your message is priceless and I thank you for it. Your father was one of a kind and we were so fortunate to be a part of his life. Don't you just love him! Thank *you for thinking that I am coping. It isn't easy, is it? Try not to replay negatives in your mind—sometimes that's easier said than done. You were very dear to send that to me and I LOVE IT and I LOVE YOU, TOO.*

xo, your dear mother

George had died in January. Exactly nine months had passed since then, when I happened to be sitting at school, in the teachers' lunchroom.

I have no idea what the conversation was about, but someone suggested that I send an e-mail to George.

Now, you must understand that I classify myself as "computer illiterate." My computer skills consist of sending and receiving e-mail and checking out horoscope sites.

But I thought: I could do that. I could send him an e-mail. In fact, I rather loved the suggestion.

That night, at home, I sent my first message. Since I didn't know his exact location, I made up an address. I figured I should use his name, plus something to do with the fact that he was now residing in spirit. That accomplished, I wrote:

How are you? I just wanted to tell you that I miss you and I love you from my soul. Thank you for all of your help. You are THE BEST.

Peace, Joy and Aloha. Love, Betty

I read it and re-read it and pressed SEND. The date was October 21, 2002. The time was 11:54 PM. I went to bed.

The next morning, at 9:59 AM, I wrote to George again, changing the address slightly by using his initials in place of his name. In large print, I typed:

I LOVE YOU SOOOOOOOOOOOOOOO MUCH!
LOVE, BETTY

I read it, and re-read it, and, again, pressed SEND.

I may not be well-versed in computers, but I do know that if you send something to an incorrect address, the little "mailer daemon" returns it to you.

Three days went by and neither message had been returned.

It was lunch time again at school, and I mentioned that I had tried the e-mail idea. I told how I had sent two messages that hadn't returned and I figured they were floating around somewhere in cyberspace.

You should have heard the increase in noise level in the room. Everyone at once suggested that I had probably sent the messages to a registered site.

How could that be? I had made up the e-mail address. They told me, "Go back to your room. Type in www. plus the exact words you used for the e-mail computer address and see what happens."

"Good idea. I'll check it out."

Please note: at the beginning of each school year, we sign papers promising not to inappropriately use the school computers. I'm certainly safe there. I had never used my room computer for personal reasons ...

prior to that day ...

However, on this day, after I had welcomed the afternoon class, and the students were busily working, I decided to check out that web site. I sat down on the little kindergarten chair and typed in www. plus the "address."

Yep, it was a registered site, all right.

It was an "erotic art" and porn registered site, to be exact.

"Jeanine, check this out!"

"What are you doing?"

"I'm not doing anything. It's George's fault, and I know he thinks it's funny. He's the one who put the address in my brain. What's he doing in an erotic art and porn site?"

Jeanine, looking down at the screen said: "Wouldn't you think there would be angels instead of whips and chains?"

Trying to exit the site, I got in even deeper. *This is definitely not funny, George. You are in big trouble!*

A little child's voice asked, "What are you doing, Mrs. Portenlanger?"

"Nothing! Nothing! Please sit down and finish your work." A voice in my brain said, "Turn off the computer, Betty!"

Done!

After school, I went into the principal's office and explained what had happened.

"Karen, if our CEO wants to know who is fooling around with the computer in my room, it's me. I sent an e-mail to George; it never came back. I checked out the site where I sent the email; it's a registered site. It's a registered 'erotic art' and porn site to be exact and I'm going to kick George's ass when I see him, because this is his idea of a joke! I am so sorry and I don't want to be on the front page of the morning paper: 'teacher uses room computer for obscene purposes while children are present.' Please know that no child saw what was on the screen."

It goes without saying that this incident was the source of raucous laughter and uninhibited humor among my colleagues. Some of the jokes *were* quite funny, actually.

Karen was very sympathetic. And Chris helped me empty my cookies, whatever that means, and I never again used the room computer for personal reasons.

One of my daughters later astutely remarked, "Think about it Mom; who sends e-mail to a dead person?"

Nonetheless, I again wrote, although it was two months and two days before I could bring myself to send another message.

This time, on Christmas Eve day, I used my home computer, and I sent an e-mail to my own address.

Thereafter, over the time frame of a little more than one year, whenever I felt that I needed to talk to George, I would send him an e-mail.

You will see clearly how the messages change from short and tentative, building to a huge, long crescendo of total disclosures. As they come full circle on the year, they again recede in size; my emotional focus was moving back to the physical life around me.

During this whole period, as strange as it may seem, I felt as if I were communicating with him.

I *was* communicating. I was e-mailing George—e-mailing Heaven—and it served its purpose well.

He answered.

MESSAGES TO REPAIR A BROKEN HEART

What follows are some of the messages that I, and a few others, wrote. They chronicle the evolution of the repair of my broken heart.

DECEMBER 2002

TUESDAY, CHRISTMAS EVE, 2002, 8:30 AM

George dear,

I wish you a merry, merry Christmas. I love you sooooooooooooo much and I thank you for all of your gifts that you have so generously given to me over the last year. Keep on sending them. I love and treasure each one. Carol said that you can do things with computers. OK, I'm waiting for whatever. I know that you will come through. Come with me to Paulina Market and Andersonville. We will have a great time.

I'll make some tea for you tonight. I do love you.
XOXOXOXXOX, Betty

TUESDAY, CHRISTMAS EVE, 2002, 3:53 PM

You outdid yourself at Paulina Market. John and I thought you were and are FANTASTIC! Thanks a million times over!

Love, me

SUNDAY, DECEMBER 29, 2002, 9:14 AM

Georgie. How did I do today? The ham was not anywhere near as good as the ones you made, but I tried and that's the main thing, I guess. Thinking of you. Do something, anything, with this computer. PLEASE. Thanking you, in advance. I love you LOTS.

xoxxoxoxoxoxoxoxooxxoooxoxoxoooxoxoxoxoxo oxoxoxoxoxoxox, Betty

WINTER 2003

THURSDAY, JANUARY 2, 2003, 11:54 PM

Georgie Dear,

Hawaii. Here we go again. Or, should I say—here we come again... Am I excited or what? Thank you for whatever it is that you are doing. I love it all and I love you. Aloha. Kisses and hugs. Love, Betty

SATURDAY, JANUARY 4, 2003, 9:37 AM

Georgie, I need your help. Keep my mind on the straight and narrow. Help me to stay focused. I love you so very much. This is not at all easy. Give me a sign or something. Come on. Something BIGTIME. And please know that you are invited to your very own GEORGE FEST 2003.

I LOVE YOU.   Love, hugs and kisses, Betty

TUESDAY, JANUARY 7, 2003, 10:04 PM

George Dear,

I hope that you think the GEORGE FEST 2003 is a good idea. Would you PLEASE give me some type of VERY obvious sign that you like my idea? You are always so FANTASTIC about letting me know how you feel and I am extremely grateful. THANK YOU, THANK YOU, THANK YOU!

It will be a good celebration of the life and times of someone who simply cannot be replaced. You know that I miss you more than anything and I LOVE YOU with all my heart and soul and mind. I cannot believe that a year has passed. How have I survived? I have survived only because you have been with me every step of the way. You are my life and I am grateful.

I love you, Georgie, and I miss you dreadfully. Send me a sign. PLEASE.

Love, me

WEDNESDAY, JANUARY 8, 2003, 4:52 PM

GEORGIE—

I need a sign, kind of right now. Something. Anything. I love you.

Am I going to be OK? I LOVE YOU.

Love, me

THURSDAY, JANUARY 9, 2003, 7:08 PM

George,

How can I go on without being with you? Maybe you can see me, but I can't see you or hear you or anything concrete and I get very sad at times. I know that we are doing a pretty good job at connecting, but I still wish with all my heart that I could hold you and that you could hold me. AND I wish that I could hear you say something outrageous. I love you and I will forever and ever and ever. Next time, could we PLEASE sign a contract that keeps us together for a very LOOOOOONG, healthy and happy life. This time was waaaaaaaaaaaaaaaaaaaaaaaaaaaaaay to short. I love and miss you. Send me a BIGTIME sign.

I love you. Love, Betty

SATURDAY, JANUARY 11, 2003, 3:38 PM

Dear, Dear George,

Do I love you? YES, I DO. Did I tell you that when you were here? I think that I did. Well, I loved you then and I love you now. Please be with me this afternoon. And, throughout the whole day. I love connecting with you and I would like a good, in your face, message sometime today.

OK, I'm off to other things. I'll check in later. You know where to find me, so give me a HUGE message. A subtle one would be great, too. THANKS.

I LOVE YOU. Love, me

SUNDAY, JANUARY 12, 2003, 11:01 PM

OK George,

This is going to be one hell of a week if I keep on crying every other minute. I'm not going to last. So, could you please help me with this? Thanks.

Don't you love it that Mary Kay is going to Ireland and I am going to visit her and that Jenna is in her class? I love you. Love, me

WEDNESDAY, JANUARY 15, 2003, 8:27 PM

Georgie Dear,

I'm going to Key West and I can't wait. Thank you for letting me be able to do all of this. I love you for that and for a thousand other reasons. This is really quite bizarre, but I am loving the connection. Thank you for the electric waves.

Are they ever going to connect the electricity? What's up with that? Maybe I should call again. Should I? Give me a sign on that one. Thanks.

Connect with me some more. I LOVE YOU. Love, me

SATURDAY, JANUARY 18, 2003, 10:18 AM

My dearest Georgie,

Why is my aura shrinking??!! Wouldn't it be fun to go across the ocean like you always wanted to do? Now that I agree to do it, you cut out on me. Perhaps I will go by myself. I think that I could do it. Don't you? Send me a fantastic connection today. PLEASE. THANK YOU.

I LOVE YOU LOTS AND LOTS AND LOTS AND LOTS. xoxoxoxoox, Betty

MONDAY, JANUARY 20, 2003, 5:48 PM

Dear, Dear George.

I am asking you to PLEASE, PLEASE, PLEASE come to our GEORGE FEST 2003.

It would just be the MOST fantastic thing if you could do something that would blow everyone away. Come on, Georgie. You can do it.

I LOVE YOU. You are my soul mate, soul friend and soul partner. xoxox, Betty

TUESDAY, JANUARY 21, 2003, 9:15 AM

George,

I am counting on your help today. I will need MASSIVE doses of your energy and love. I am thanking you in advance. Please, if you have the time, come to your party tonight. It won't be the same without you.

Do I really need a cat? I don't think so either.

I love you. Love, Betty

TUESDAY, JANUARY 21, 2003, 11:50 PM

Well George, we did it. Thank you for all of your help,

AND, thanks for ringing the bell at the perfect time. I know that you were here.

I wish with all my heart that we never ever had to have a GEORGE FEST. I liked it much better when we just had you! I love you.

WEDNESDAY, JANUARY 22, 2003, 7:14 AM

To Kate

From me

Dear, Dear Katie,

THANK YOU for everything you did to make yesterday a success. I think that it went very well. ALWAYS remember that your father thought you were FANTASTIC. He still does.

Enjoy this day.   Love, your dear mother

To Moll

From me

Wednesday, January 22, 2003, 7:16 AM

Dear, Dear Margaret,

THANK YOU for everything you did to make yesterday a success. I think that it went very well. ALWAYS remember that your father thought you were FANTASTIC. He still does.

Enjoy this day.   Love, your dear mother

Traveling with George

FRIDAY, JANUARY 24, 2003, 8:37 PM

Georgie, Georgie

It is soooooooooooooo cold and I am very glad to be home for the week-end. Do you think that I should call Joe and ask him if I have to do something special with the water pipes for the outside faucets? Please don't let anything freeze and burst. I know that you will keep everything in good shape. Thanks, in advance, for all of the help you are sending. Are you just the best there is or ever was or ever will be? YES, you are and I love you for being you.

I love you so very, very, VERY much. Peace, joy, love and abundance, Betty

PS: What was that noise at 11:00 the other night? Moll and I could not find anything.

SUNDAY, JANUARY 26, 2003, 4:58 PM

George,

I have just finished getting everything together to do the income tax and I think that I'm in pretty good shape. I just have to wait to see how much will be added to the income from that one annuity that I put into my name and they gave it to me as a pay-out and then they couldn't reverse it. Who cares at this point. I just wish that you were here. I love you and now I am feeling so very sad because I have come through a whole year without you and I ABSOLUTELY HATE IT. I LOVE YOU, but I ABSOLUTELY HATE this going along my journey without you. You are terribly missed. Come back. PLEASE.

I love you—love, Betty

TUESDAY, JANUARY 28, 2003, 5:26 PM

Oh George, you're never going to believe this!

I just finished doing a preliminary job on the income taxes. I CANNOT believe that I am going to have to come up with !!,000 fricken more dollars than I have already paid. It is nice to live in this marvelous country and I am grateful that I do AND I am thankful that you built this marvelous house for me, but come on—do you realize how many airplane tickets that money could buy?! OK George, this is where you come in. I need the money, I don't want to take it out of any account and I am wondering how it is going to appear. I have no doubt that it will just show up, but I was wondering how in the world are you going to make it turn up? Thanking you, in advance, for your creativity.

I love you, love you, LOVE YOU.

Peace to us all, Betty.

WEDNESDAY, JANUARY 29, 2003, 6:13 PM

Dear George,

Last night I did the real figuring on the taxes and we never had to pay the exorbitant amount that I am going to have to pay. I couldn't stand it and so I went out to shovel the snow. How did you do the shoveling for so many years? And you did much more than I have to do. Thank you for having done it year after year after year. Anyway, I was trying to figure out a way to cheat BIGTIME (not really) and avoid going to prison. It's all monopoly money anyway, but it still is a WHOLE lot of monopoly money.

Today I have a terrible wave of sadness coming over me and I think that I am not going to make it for the long haul. I miss you terribly and I think that I give up. I simply give up. I don't want to go on, but I don't have any idea how to take my life. Maybe I could just go to sleep and never wake up. At least never wake up in this lifetime. How can I even say that when I have so much to live for? It's just that I miss you. This is not easy. You'd hate it. I love you, Betty

THURSDAY, JANUARY 30, 2003, 5:50 PM

Georgie Dear,

I am not used to having dark thoughts. I absolutely hate them. So, I am not going to go there again. Chuck said that I am in a tunnel that I entered a year ago and I will come out and the sun will shine again. Poor Maureen and Jeanine! They are so very dear and I am EXTREMELY grateful that they are in my life. What would I ever do if I didn't have them to share my thoughts/feelings with? I have an incredible support team. AND, you are the team leader. I MUST read the "NOW" book. I am sabotaging my progress by forgetting to concentrate on the BIG picture. But you were my picture and now things are out of focus. Remember when you were wearing my glasses and thought that you were going blind? That's what it is sort of like. Except, that was funny and this definitely is not.

Today Scott's little boy registered for my next years kindergarten class. Made me feel good. It goes without saying that I love you. But, I need to say it anyway. I LOVE YOU! Keep the messages coming. I need, want and live for them. xo, Betty

THURSDAY, JANUARY 30, 2003, 6:02 PM

George,

Forgot to include this in the last message. Part of my problem, I think, is that I haven't been able to go for walks around the park because of the cold, cold weather. I miss the exercise AND the fresh air to clear my thoughts. Maybe I'll get the rebounder up and jump on that for awhile. Bounce any stupid thoughts out of my mind.

Love you LOTS! Betty

WEDNESDAY, FEBRUARY 5, 2003, 6:11 PM

Hi George,

I am tired today. There never seems to be time just to sit and do NOTHING. Kate called this morning and asked if we could get together on Sunday. She would like me to meet her new friend. I can't wait and I think that we will all be going out to dinner. I still have a very difficult time around cooking. You always did such a marvelous job of it and when it comes to "kitchen" things I go into deep distress. You are missed in so many areas. Your kitchen skills are not replaceable. In several other areas you are not replaceable either. I love, love, love you. I hope that you are having a marvelous time soaring around us and the Universe. I miss you.

Joy to the fishes in the deep blue sea, joy to you and me. Love, Betty

WEDNESDAY, FEBRUARY 12 2003, 2:21 PM

Georgie, Georgie, Georgie,

It has been a while since I've written. Time just evaporates. I am enjoying the day off compliments of Abraham Lincoln.

We had dinner with Kate and her friend the other evening and it was a very nice time. You would like him, but then, you probably already know him. He would have enjoyed meeting you and I would have loved to have had you there with me. This is not easy. I know there is still a lot of history to be written for our little family and how I wish that you were here to share in the journey with me. I REALLY KNOW that you are sharing it with us. I just wish that I could see you and hear your wise and witty comments along the way.

Went to the Mind, Body, Spirit Fair the other day and it was too funny that you sent that girl into the mix. Did she have to be from St. Benedict's High School, your alma mater? Too funny! I got the message. AND, how nice that you are on the Bardo Plane. I am reading up on it. Don't know if I can understand it all, though.

Well, I am definitely looking forward to the Hawaii trip. Great job sending the PELE card my way.

I LOOOOOOOVE you so much. Your messages are the greatest and I thank you for sending them. You know that I would not be making it if it were not for inside jokes.

Have fun and please keep the vibes coming. YOU ARE FANTASTIC!!!!!!!

I love you. Yes, I do. Love, Betty

SUNDAY, FEBRUARY 16, 2003, 9:34 PM

Dear George,

Could you please help out Moll. She is in deep distress regarding her long work hours. Hopefully, she will be able to work into a new situation soon. This is not a good match for her. She is so dear and I absolutely hate to see her this unhappy. Thanks for all of your help here, as well. This is a long week-end and it will be so sad to go to Nora's funeral. What a loss for all of us; not to mention the loss for her family. Things are difficult to figure out from this vantage point. But, I'm trying. I love you for your help. Send me a sign. I ALWAYS love your messages. One last thing, I'm going to visit schools near Kona and I can't wait. Actually, I can't wait to get back there to the warmth and all of Hawaii. Am I supposed to head in that direction for part of my life journey? Help me out with this one.

Well, HAPPY VALENTINE'S DAY. I was remembering when we were on Abaco. I love you and thank you for all of the wonderful trips that we went on.

PEACE to you my dear, dear Georgie   Love, Betty

SATURDAY, FEBRUARY 22, 2003, 9:29 AM

George Dear,

This has been a VERY hectic week and I would love to hear what you would have to say about all of the stuff that is taking place. Thursday was absolutely horrible. I fought with Moll, my mother (I couldn't make her understand something), and, on the verge, with Kate.

I abhor dissension. Nothing in the world is worth it. And it wasn't even a full moon!

Poor Moll is not at all happy about her job situation and hopefully, she will be able to move into something more agreeable. The poor dear is working so very hard AND long. She deserves a break. Even though it is rare, you know how it is when she cries. It just breaks my heart when she says: "I wish Dad were here. He'd know what to tell me." That is simply more than I can bear. I can take care of my own heart, but when hers breaks, it devastates me.

In two weeks, at this very moment, we will be on a plane heading to Hawaii and I can't wait to see and feel and smell the ocean. I know that you can go any moment you choose, but I am limited. Don't you just love it there? Thank you for sending us in that direction.

Tomorrow I am calling to connect with Carol. Please have some input. I know you will and I can't wait to hear it. I love you more than life itself and Elizabeth Barrett Browning was correct about loving someone more after death. I NEVER would have thought that it was possible. Why didn't I know this when I could see you? I think that you knew so much. Please forgive me for being such a dunce about things. You are so very dear to me. I need a VERY visible sign today. And, I thank you, in advance, for whatever surprise you are going to send.

I am so very glad that we are eternally connected. I could not survive if I didn't know that. I love you LOTS! And LOTS! And LOTS! Peace to you, my Anam Cara

FRIDAY, MARCH 7, 2003, 4:48 PM

Georgie Dear,

Life is just too, too busy. I have no idea where the time goes, but it just evaporates and I am welcoming the time that I will have in Hawaii to simply slow down and be. I miss communicating with you and I am so looking forward to connecting with you.

Tomorrow, Kate, Moll and I leave at 7:00am. I have covered the bases with my mother. I think we're all set. Thanks for the huge/hugh joke with Marty. I know that it was your way of saying "hello" to him. Very funny making me look "stoopud." I can't wait for the ocean experience. Please join us. I know that you will. Please let me be fully aware of your wonderful messages. I am expecting great fun. I know that you will do your best to be with us and I thank you from the bottom of my heart. This is difficult at times (actually when I think about it, it is difficult all of the time). I miss you terribly. I won't get sad. I'll just concentrate on the wild donkeys, the Dragonfly Ranch, St. Benedict's Church, the volcano and the visit with Alice on Oahu. I'll see you there. I know you are with me every step of the way. I love you. God, how I love you. I miss you so much. YOU BETTER SEND ME SOME IN YOUR FACE MESSAGES OR I WILL NOT SURVIVE!

Thank you, George. You are too wonderful. Peace, Joy, Love and Abundance, Betty

PS Were we really Berbers?

SPRING 2003

WEDNESDAY, APRIL 2, 2003, 7:19 PM

Dear, Dear Georgie,

It has been almost a month since I last wrote. You are on my mind and in my head and heart CONSTANTLY. Hawaii was just wonderful and unbelievable. The whales were THE BEST. I know that you were instrumental in sending them to entertain us and you were also there to keep us safe. But really George—only one life vest! The Buddhist Temple was spectacular and the visit with Alice delightful.

I think that I will be going to California to meet Carol this summer. It would be fun to see Joan and Lois and Carol. PLEASE, PLEASE say that you will be there. I know that you will and that I don't even have to ask. I love you for that!! Where else will I be going? I have no idea, but I know that you will send me on some type of fantastic adventure. How about Bermuda? Don't you think that that sounds like a good idea? I do. Give me some direction or better yet just lead the way. I'm tired of making decisions.

Joe fixed my mother's doorknob and locks today AND the light fixture in the den. How nice to have that all taken care of. Well George dear, I am going to watch some TV. I am very tired today and somewhat sad. I know why I am sad. Tomorrow is my birthday and I wish that I could just see you and hold you and have you give me a wonderful hug. I miss your beautiful arms more than you can possibly imagine. I love you George. I always have and I always will. God, I love you. I know that I was deeply loved and that I still am and for that I am tremendously grateful. Be with

me Georgie; I love you more than life itself. *PEACE.*
Love, Betty

THURSDAY, APRIL 10, 2003, 4:46 PM

George Dear,

I'm thinking that this is going to be a long road that I'm on without you where I can see you. Once again, I am thinking—am I going to make it? I know that I have no choice but to forge ahead, but it really is definitely not as much fun as when I could hear all of your "over the top" comments and outrageously witty sayings. I miss that AND you.

On Saturday I leave for Key West and our favorite hotel. It goes without saying that I need you to go with me. Please make it VERY evident that you are there with me. I am thanking you, IN ADVANCE, for all of the signals that you will most surely send.

Margaret told them at work today that she has accepted a new position. I know that they are sorry to have her leave. Kate has had several people at her job "let go" and that has made her very sad. She moves back into her old apartment building at the end of this month. Do you think that it will be difficult for me to go back there? I will probably see you there the first couple of times that I return.

Looking forward to this summer. Do you think that I should go to Bermuda? Maybe stay at the "Waterloo." I am, for certain, going to California to meet Carol. So, put in your reservation early. Be there with me. I can't wait to meet her AND see you. Then Joan and Lois and I are going to get together. I am not going to Effingham because the time is simply non-existent. The summer is evaporating and it isn't even here.

You are too, too dear. I love you so f'n much. I've got to start packing for the trip. I love you Georgie. I always have and I always will. You are so dear to me. Thank you for being you. Next time, could we PLEASE plan this out for a longer ride? I LOVE YOU. Please be with me Georgie. I know that you are, but I just had to ask.

xoxoxxooxoxoxox, me

WEDNESDAY, APRIL 23, 2003, 6:29 PM

George Dear,

I simply love Key West. Now I know what I will do after I quit work. I am going to have a little act on the pier, at sunset. Really, I think that I could do it and have fun AND make some money. I know that you think that I won't get a chance to do it, but I can hear you say—"if you want to do that, go right ahead." The "Jesus went with Bethany to the twelve" thing was too, too funny. And the fact that I was awakened at 4AM, after sleeping through two alarms, was simply awesome. Thank you. Never would I have made the plane. I am so very grateful.

It was fun to have lunch with Cathleen and Rene and Mary. Almost as if I live there and was welcoming guests. It was just like the time Joe and Joanne came to visit. I can't believe that it has taken me a year to realize that I have been living in a fog. I thought that I was functioning, but I really wasn't. Just now, I am beginning to feel as if I am getting my life back on track. Thank you for your incredible help.

Yesterday, Margaret said: "Would the two of you please get out of my room." I absolutely loved it!

Take care, George. Please keep sending your guidance and love and messages. And please let me be aware of and open to them. I need, want and love them. And, I love you—now and forever. I am so grateful for you. Thank you a million times over. xo, me

FRIDAY, MAY 2, 2003, 6:09 PM

Geo, Geo, Geo,

It is delightful to be home. Do you think that I could get used to being a hermit? No, you're right. I'd probably hate it after a little bit, but sometimes I'd love to give it a try.

This has been a hectic week and I know that you have helped me get through it. THANK YOU!! I really hope that my mother gets complete relief from her pain. Things worked out well when she had to go to the hospital for her outpatient treatment. Moll was able to take her, I left work early and then Kate stopped by and was able to help get her home and pick up her medicine. Not bad.

Today is Margaret's last day at the college and I hope that it went well. She is so cute—she wrote notes to everyone and put them in the mailboxes. Kate moved back to the building where you last carried up the suitcases. She can't fit the sofa—yes, that sofa—into the apartment, so it is in our garage. The new place was such a mess that they had to send in a special cleaning crew to fix it up. She's going back there today to get things straightened up.

We have had some big storms this week and the gutter on the front of the house had been clogged with seeds from the maple tree. It's quite a mess. Do you think that I should get leaf guards or would they be a bigger problem than the seeds? Please let me know. I love, love, love you.

When I was looking at the Egyptian exhibit at the museum last Sunday, I was overwhelmed with sadness. The Egyptians were so respectful of their dead. By contrast, I felt horrible about not giving you the proper send-off at the "moment of impact" when your spirit left your body. I am so very sorry. Please say that you forgive me. I was in shock and had no idea what was going on. I know that you would say that it's all right, but I just wish that I had been more aware and that I would have said a prayer or something religious at the time. In my defense I can only say that, when I was standing in the street at the accident scene, I didn't want to believe that you were dead.

I love you George and while I think that I am doing pretty good, please know that I miss you terribly and that I wish you were in your body so that I could give you a BIG hug and have you hold me. I miss you and love you and wish that I could see you.

I love you. Thank you for being so dear. Please, could you send a HUGE in your face message? I need it, BIGTIME. Thanking you, in advance. I LOVE YOU.

Love, Betty

SUNDAY, MAY 18, 2003, 9:28 PM

My Dear, Dear Georgie,

Don't you just LOVE the garden? Margaret has done so much work and it is taking shape. Today she planted 12 tomato plants and put flowers in your old grill. It is a delight to see her working out there. I know that she feels a closeness to you and that her work is a tribute to you. Plus, the Tibetan Peace Flags that she bought at the museum really add color and interest. Also, the quilt that she made from your shirts is priceless. I want one and this summer I am going to make one for myself. I love it.

Tomorrow she begins her new job. I suggested that she take their health insurance and not keep the interim policy. What do you think? Her birthday is Thursday. Hope to "see" you at the celebration.

Kate called on her way home from St. Louis. She went to see the Cubs play. Good old Cubbies

The Memorial Day party is taking shape. I'm having sloppy joes. Sorry, but I just can't do an "Effingham." I think that I'll ask Joe or Mike or Kenneth to help me figure out how to hang up that HUGE, BEAUTIFUL vine wreath that you made for me. It was on the lantern, but since the screen door has been put on, it won't fit. I thought of putting a nail into the siding, but re-thought and figured you would like me to get some "expert" advice. So, I am waiting. Didn't Joe do a great job with the gutter guards? Yes, he did.

I know that you were with us at the Mass of Remembrance at the hospital yesterday. It really was beautiful and it meant a great deal to me. Hope you don't mind that it involved two of your most favorite (NOT) institutions at once. I just wish that I didn't have a reason to attend. I love you and this all stinks.

Things are going along and I think that you would tell me that I am doing a pretty good job of it, but it isn't easy and I miss you terribly. I want to hug you and I want you to hug me. To paraphrase Elizabeth Barrett Browning: How do I MISS you, let me count the ways... Thank you a million times over for who you were, who you are and who you will always be. I love you Georgie and I ABSOLUTELY HATE this part of my life journey. It was so much more fun and comforting and beautiful to have you as my traveling companion. Haunt me, I need it.

Be well. I love you dearly. Love, Betty

PS: Is this electric company snafu some sort of cosmic joke that you are playing or what is going on? It is funny, but really, enough is enough. How HUGE is the bill going to be when they finally hook up the meter after almost two years? I love, love, love you.

THURSDAY, JUNE 5, 2003, 7:56 PM

Dear, Dear Georgie,

So much has happened since I last wrote to you. I know that you have kept tabs, but I just have to put it down on paper.

So, here goes—my mother decided to sell her car. Yes, the phantom car. Ellen's family bought it for her sister, Laurie. Thank you for your help. I think that the car is happy about its new family. We had a fabulous Memorial Day and I made great sloppy joes from the beginning and not from a can. They just needed some extra zip and I wished that you were here to give me the secret of what it was that needed to be added to the mix. Bought 2 cans of Manwich and added it to the batch and they were DELICIOUS, if I do say so myself. Everyone brought great contributions. I ate some of the salads on the following Thursday evening and got ptomaine —————-it was so very awful that I wanted to die. I was in bed for three days and I was calling you names. If you had been here you would have said: "Don't eat that Betty, throw it away." Man, was I ever sick! Never again. Actually, I think that you were behind it to give me some much needed enforced relaxation. So, on second thought, thank you.

Just went to the hardware store to get some ant spray. Huge black ants are in the kitchen by the waste basket and so I came home and sprayed and sprayed and sprayed. We'll probably die and the ants will take over. Oh, ask me if I have an electric meter yet. You guessed it. NO! This really is not funny. Should I worry? Well, I'm not going to. I suppose it is somewhat funny. I know that you're the one sending answers to questions that I have, because it seems as if all of the pieces are being put into place and that the answers are just appearing. I know that it is all of your doing and I am most grateful. When I have time, I really must get this vacation finalized. I need your help on that one. And, I need your help on where I am going to live—the coast or an island or wherever. HELP. Your guidance is appreciated.

Thank goodness that I didn't have a missing (for real) child at school yesterday. There have been some awfully strange things going on lately. Please take care of Kate and Moll. You know what they need. Spin them in the right direction. Don't spin me. Just be there and guide me. I'm starting to get a wave of sadness come over me and if I let it, I will begin to sob. I miss you. Looking at the vacation and family videos is such a vivid reminder of how wonderful things were in our lives. Did I thank you when you were here? I know I did, but did you fully realize just how much I loved you and that I still love you and I will love you for all of eternity?

I am so fortunate. What if I were in some rotten soul family? God, how I love you. And, God, how I miss you. At this point I am doing what Kate and Moll hate. It's when I do what they call the "waaa, waaa" stuff. But, I can't help it. You wouldn't be liking this

185

too much, Georgie. What is the next mission that I am supposed to accomplish in this life and will I know what it is when it is looking me in the face? I must close, 'cause I have to do some school stuff. A week and a half left.

Do you think that I am going to make it 'til summer vacation? Wish you were here so that I could hear your hilarious comments about the news—Sosa's bat for one thing. You were so incredibly funny. Why did you choose to bail? COME ON. Help me connect. You can do it and I think that I could do it, with your help. Let's go for it. Thank you my dear, dear George. I LOVE YOU xo, me

FRIDAY, JUNE 13, 2003, 7:55 PM

Georgie, Georgie, Georgie,

Tomorrow is a full moon and I think that it is affecting everyone and everything! Just received a phone call from Carol and I simply cannot wait to meet her in July. I am so very excited and I am TOTALLY expecting you to show up BIG TIME. Help me get it together so that I can see you, too. I CAN'T WAIT!!

Do you believe he had a heart attack two days ago. You would be so proud of me for the distance that I have traveled emotionally. No anger or bad thoughts or ill will or crying. Just sincere, good, kind wishes that he would get better in no time at all. It was a marvelous feeling.

I have traveled a huge distance since you have been gone and I know that you are responsible for my growth. I am so very glad that his dysfunction is out of my life and I apologize, once again, for ever introducing it into our family. Please, please, please forgive me for that one. I know you do, but what a stupid, stupid fool I was. Never again will I waste time and energy. I thank you profusely. You are fantastic.

Also, Ron had a stroke and Phil cut his thumb and index finger almost off when he was doing some woodworking. What an awful week.

You are so very dear and God, how I love, love, love you. Get ready for Tahoe and thereabouts. Won't we have a blast? Thank you, in advance, for all of the experiences that you are going to give us.

Have to go and do some school stuff. Next week it is OVER and while I loved this year, it has been busy working with 64 children. But, I made it and it wouldn't have been possible if not for Jeanine. She is so great.

Who are we all? Send me some messages. I feel as if you are really feeding me info at a rapid rate. I f-'in love you. Gotta go. Come with me. I truly love you and feel your love surround me and I am most grateful. I love you, Georgie. I do, I do, I do.

SUMMER 2003

MONDAY, JUNE 23, 2003, 4:14 PM

Dear George,

Well, Jeanine and I did it! The classroom is completely clean and the records are done and everything is ready at school for the summer. Today it was 90 degrees in there and it was a bit hot, but we finished EVERYTHING and it feels fantastic.

Now, if I could only get our basement cleaned. Will you please help me? Thanks, I knew you would. I think that I am going to get some more of the plastic shelving units from the Hardware Store and that should put my mind at ease when it rains. Thank you a million times over for this beautiful house. I have the air conditioner running and it feels so very cool. I am extremely sorry that you had to live without it in the other house. How did we do it? I know. We survived because we did it together. I love you for that and for a thousand/million other reasons.

God, Georgie—how am I ever going to do this for the long haul? I miss you terribly. I know that you are right here, but I wish that I could just see you and feel you. This is difficult and I am not liking this at the moment. I feel like that little man you saw in the coffee shop. The one whose wife had died and he said to his friend: "I am lost without her." Well George, I know exactly how he feels. If anyone were to ask me, I would say: I am lost without him.

I am happy to be out for the summer and I am grateful to Jeanine and Trish for telling me NOT to send the note. It would have been misconstrued and that would be awful. Thank you for nailing my feet to the street and for not letting me be pressured into going to visit him. I DO NOT ever need to have him cross my line of vision again in this lifetime. I am doing just fine, thank you. Actually, THANK YOU! I love you, I love you, I LOVE YOU.

And I love your big old "Popeye arms" and everything else big about you. Keep on helping me. I simply could not go on without it. I love you dearly and I know that I will see you again. I just wish that you could come back this instant and we could go together to Alice's. I would love to swim off her beach with you. Please be there with me. Bye for now, George. I love you dearly.

SUNDAY, JUNE 29, 2003, 6:14 PM

Georgie,

I rearranged the back porch. Your gorgeous vine wreath is now in the perfect spot. Is that why it fell off of the wall? Now I can see it when I look out of the kitchen window. Thank you for the idea.

Did I tell you that I think that I broke my toe? At this point it is purple and hurting. Moll is so cute. Her suggestion is to just tape it to another toe and deal with it. Aren't you glad we paid $125,000 for her education? Great return on our investment. At the moment she is working a lacrosse game in Wilmette. College kids against 40-year-old dudes. Should be fun, with lots of people getting hurt. Good luck, Moll.

Kate is in Boston. I was going to go to a "Dream Spirits Fair" in Evanston, but instead, I opted to work in the yard and finish reading "The Lovely Bones." I'm so glad that I did that. Is it anything like in the book? I HOPE SO. I really hope so. I'm wearing your shirt today because I wanted you to be working in the yard with me. I love the shirt and you. Thank you for the visit yesterday. It keeps me alive.

I love you dearly and I am so looking forward to this vacation and especially meeting Carol. PLEASE be there with me. I know that you will, but it would be too, too awesome if you did something BIGTIME and "in your face." It would be marvelous if you did one of your subtle, but over the top messages, as well. Those are so you and SO appreciated. I love you dearly. And, I miss you more than anything. I love you. I love you. I love you.

Thank you for taking such good care of us. You are

unbelievable. God, you were and are the best. Bye, Georgie. I love you.

xoxoxoxxoxoxoxoxoxooxoxoxxoxoxo, me

THURSDAY, JULY 10, 2003, 2:42 PM

George, George, George,

Just returned from a walk to the framing store. I took that darling Carl Larsson picture that you liked, to be framed. I think that it will be happy to be up and out of the basement. I'm going to hang it in the kitchen above the old bookcase. I've taken the picture that was there and put it in the front hall. Looks quite nice.

On the way back home, I stopped at the hot dog stand and had a hot dog in your honor. No wonder you left this dimension! How could you eat those things?? Also had a tamale. They have changed and now they are packaged 4 small ones to an order, instead of one large one. Not bad. Then I walked home—I agree with Maxine, I don't like walking over the expressway, either.

Next week we leave for Tahoe. I am asking the Universe to help me win BIGTIME at the slots. That would be such fun. Then I could help Kate with her condo wish. Maybe you could lend a hand with that, too. I know that it will work out. Thanking you, in advance.

Isn't it fun that Paul is in Hawaii? He and Alice and I are going to Chinatown and out to eat. I can't wait to see him.

I love you Georgie and I miss seeing you. When I am with Carol, PLEEEEEEEEASE make yourself known. I need that and I would love it so much. Do something totally you. It will be interesting to see *what actually takes place. Thank you for being with Margaret at the energy healing last night. That was wild. Thank you for helping Kate. She is in need and deserving of your guidance. ME TOO. AND, help me with whatever is going on with my mother. Many thanks. I am sorry that we are keeping you so busy. Do you ever get to do what you want to do? What you are supposed to do?*

See you later, Georgie. I love you more than anything. God, how I love you!!! Thank you for being there, here and everywhere.

xoxooxoxo, me

FRIDAY, AUGUST 8, 2003, 12:36 PM

George, Dear, Dear George,

Well my body has returned to Chicago, but my mind and heart and spirit are elsewhere. What an OUTSTANDING three weeks. I simply love vacations. I love being home, but I do love to travel. Next time, I am NOT taking that HUGE suitcase. I had to pay $25, two times, because it was overweight. PLUS, it kind of has bad vibes attached to it and so I am forever and ever going to use your new one.

OK, now to the important stuff. You REALLY outdid yourself BIGTIME in Old Town San Diego. Beth and Carol and Ron and I were totally blown away. You have no idea, well you probably do have a very good idea, how incredible that experience was to all of us. I am still aghast at the enormity of it all. You are too, too much and I thank you over and over and over again. HOW DO/DID YOU DO THAT? And the music at Lake Tahoe AND the movie in Honolulu and the meeting at Alice's.

How can I ever repay you for all of the fantastic, out of this world connections? I need them and want them desperately. I am so grateful for your beautiful help. It makes me cry to think of all of the help that you are giving to me and there is absolutely no way that I can hold you and let you know how grateful I am and how much I love you. I trust that you realize it, but this brain wave stuff is difficult for me. I liked the physicalness so much better. Plus, I can't see you. I'm not having much luck with how Carol told me to do it. Maybe I haven't given it enough time or practice. This is not easy—going through life with an invisible partner. I love it, but it certainly is strange. I'm not complaining. I'll take it. It would be unbearable if you weren't around. How would I ever, ever survive? God, how I looooooooove you.

Kate, Moll and I had a wonderful time with Lois in Tahoe. I can't believe that they climbed the mountain at Squaw Valley. Joan and Don are the best, what fun in California; Paul was so marvelous to share his time with me in Honolulu—I never really knew him before and we had a blast; Alice was a dear and it was good to end the connection with our mutual friend (I hadn't felt right about leaving so abruptly last November). I thought of the title of my book as I was walking along her beach one day.

Next week, I am definitely going to get to the basement. It has got to be pulled together. Like I really want to do that. Well, yes, I really do want to get to that task. Help me, will you please? I know that you will. So, thank you for what you will provide.

That's about it. I love you and I always will. Now I fully understand the meaning of the poem: "Time Is." Remember the one where I would ask you over and over again: "What does this mean, George?" Well, now I know exactly what the line — "for those who

Messages to Repair a Broken Heart

love, time is eternity" — means and I am so comforted by the thought. I love you, but I do miss you. If I really stopped to think about how much I miss you I could not go on. So, I just go on. I love you more than ever and I am so blessed to know that you love me, too. Enjoy whatever it is that you are doing. I am so proud of you. You are in my heart ALL OF THE TIME.

xoxoxoxoxoxoxoxooxoxox, Betty

SATURDAY, AUGUST 16, 2003, 3:11 PM

George Dear,

I am trying to ignore the fact that the summer is dwindling FAST. There seems to be something to do almost every day before school begins. While I am delighted to have things to do, I wish that I could just be a bit bored. I know that you used to get nuts when I said that I wished I had time to be bored. You always thought "who would want to be bored?" Well, I just wish that the whirlwind would calm down a little. If it ever did calm down, I would probably hate it.

I am very excited about my "book." Lois is going to write an introduction and so is Kathi. My notes and writings will take forever to organize, but I don't care. I really want to do this. It is more for me than for anyone else. You are ALWAYS welcome to send more material for this effort. I love to "hear" from you.

I passed the message on to Jeanine about getting her car checked. Well, I guess that I didn't tell her soon enough, because her car broke down yesterday. Thanks for trying.

My "third eye" massage was wonderful. I wasn't expecting the message that came through. Seems I am realizing that I need to do some Spring cleaning of friends. Is this the by-product of death? You appear to be realigning my directions. I am getting the message and I am delighted in the method. I just need to be quiet and realize the outcomes. One time I said, "Don't spin me in any new directions." Well, I have no idea where, how or when I need to be spun. So have at it. I am learning to LOVE the new direction and the subtle process.

Kathi and I were in the store the other day and the radio played two songs before we left—one that was meaningful for me and one that was meaningful for her. Too, too interesting. Who did that? It freaked us out and we were so unnerved we abruptly left the store.

OK, so it wasn't the food that did you in? It was the bout you had with rheumatic fever. Therefore, I will toast you with each hot dog that I eat and I won't say rotten things when I do.

Could you please help Moll, gentle soul that she is; she needs some guidance with work issues. Thanks.

Also, should we get a dog? Or is that a dumb idea? I think that it could work. Help on that one, too.

Bye for now. I love, love, LOVE you. Why did you have to leave in order for me to begin to see things in a new and better light? Was it because I wouldn't listen to you when you were here? God, how I wish that you could just come back for a little while so that I could see you and hold you and touch those gorgeous Popeye arms. I love you, Georgie. Always have and always will.   Hugs and Kisses, Betty.

To Kate and Moll

From me

Saturday, August 30, 2003, 12:20 PM

Dear Dears,

I have been going over e-mail that I have sent to your father and I have a request to ask. If you have any thought — any thoughts at all — as to how you feel at this point in the trip, since he died, could you please put it in an e-mail and send it to me. I would like to include it in my writings. You can make it as funny or as thought-provoking as you want. It can be short or long or whatever. You can write once, or you can write anytime you think of something that you would like included. Your input would be greatly appreciated. A note to him. A note to me. A note to the Universe. Whatever. It will be fantastic. Thank you. You are both so very clever and so very smart and so very very.

Love, your dear mother

SATURDAY, AUGUST 30, 2003, 1:17 PM

George,

I think that I am ready for the school year to begin. The room is all set. The children come next Tuesday. Beth was so cute. She and Donna and I were eating at the "George Portenlanger Memorial Booth" at Nick's Drive-In and she looked right at me and said: "Do you know how well loved you are?" Not: how well loved you WERE, but how well loved you ARE. YES, I do know and it was simply wonderful to have her realize it and say it out loud. That afternoon and the next day, too, I told her how much that meant to me and how much I loved her for saying it. I am well loved. I knew it when you were here, but I didn't realize how completely well loved I was. It is for eternity and that is awesome. I LOVE YOU.

Well, this is so OVER THE TOP, but I am going back to Hawaii in November. I think that Kate is going to go with me. Moll isn't going; she is going to Key West with me in the Spring. Is this just too, too excessive? Let me know your opinion. People will think that I have really lost it. Who cares. This time I am taking your suitcase. I am so sick of lugging that other huge thing around. I'm taking the bare minimum. It should be a great experiment. Maybe I will skip Oahu and just go to Kona. I was thinking of going to the volcano and staying at the Volcano House. Good idea? Yes? No?

I spent the morning checking all of the mail that I have sent you. It is interesting to go back and see the distance that I have traveled. Remember the first message I sent to that "address" that I made up? That was really NOT funny George. How could you have let me do that and what were you doing in that site in the first place. Funny, George. Really funny.

I have decided that I am not going to have Thanksgiving this year. I just can't do it. Last year it was necessary. I loved doing it, but afterwards the next two days were an emotional disaster for me. Hope that everyone understands. They will. Had the apple tree and the black walnut tree trimmed. I think that the tree at the corner of the house has to come down. When Marty has his tree taken down, I'll ask those guys to take this one down. I am calling the electric company next week. Talk about excessive! This is nuts. Almost two years and still no meter. What are you doing Geo? Is this your cosmic joke? I will probably go to jail. Do not pass go, do not collect $200. Go directly to jail. This really has to get settled. Also, I don't want to go through another winter without having the front door stained. I think that I can do it myself.

OK, I think that's it. Goes without saying that I love you tremendously. But I will say it anyway. I love you dearly and I thank you so very much for the help that you are showering down on all of us. Kate and Moll and I are grateful and love you beyond belief.

I love you Georgie. I love, love, love you. xo, me

From Moll

To me

Monday, September 1, 2003, 1:51 PM

i am not sure if I was supposed to address this to you or dad so...

let's see; feelings right now are somewhat the same as in 2002: annoyed, irate, angry, sad, frustrated, a sense of loss. things like that.

i absolutely hate it when people say he is in a better place and that he is with God. whatever. he should be with us.

i miss that he is not here now to deal with everything and to hear first hand about my work and to have him be the mediator, etc. i always have a sense of comfort, which i believe is him being with me and that i always know that if i am worried about or concerned about something everything will work out and be OK.

when you say trip, i am not sure if i like that or not. a trip is supposed to be a vacation, a fun time and this is far from it. journey fits the same as trip, so i would use neither of those. i am not sure what i would call it. this whole situation (better word) has allowed me to not care so much about the little things, which is great and makes me more aware of the world around me and what should be important in life. i don't have to do anything i do not want to. life is short. you should do what you want to do. that is it for now. :) Mol

From Kate
To me

Monday, September 15, 2003, 7:37 PM

Hi Ma —

Hope you are feeling better today... we are definitely getting you a damn cell phone...

I asked for the days off for Hawaii so I am in like Flynn.

Also, can you tell dad Hi. And how's it goin' pal?

I am still working on getting an "f'in hobby," but I suppose if I did, then I

wouldn't be Kate.

Love to Dad.

K

FALL 2003

SATURDAY, OCTOBER 18, 2003, 10:18 PM

My dear, dear, dear George,

Time evaporates and it seems like ages since I last wrote to you. So much has happened and so much keeps happening that I am amazed at the pace and the wealth of information. It is as if I am hurtling through time and space. Did you have to leave so that I could grow and change? I am definitely not the same person

I was when you were here. I think that I am much nicer and wiser and feel as if I am "waking up." You always said that about the Buddha being "awake" and I had no clue. I now understand. Thank you for your guidance. I am so very sorry that I wasn't on the "same page" as you were. You were always so extremely patient and kind. God George, how I loved you then and how I love you all the more now. It is such an indescribable, comforting feeling. How blessed and fortunate I am. I love you.

Carol Dirck is coming November 6, 7 and 8. I CAN NOT WAIT. Please be with us when she is here. I don't know why I even ask, because I know that you wouldn't miss it for the world. THANK YOU for whatever it is that you are going to do. I am smiling just thinking about it. May I request a great experience? Come on, you can do it.

What did you do to get me to buy that book? Thank you for showing Maureen her pictures and thank you for the book, but most of all THANK YOU for the stealth bomber images in our pictures. I ABSOLUTELY LOVE IT!! How did/do you do that? And then, to top it off, thank you for showing Jeanine the angel artist. You are too, too wild. I can't wait to show Carol.

Well, we have an electric meter. The mix-up was all so unnecessary. I can't wait to see how it all ends. Turn theirs off, please. Did I do a good job on the front door? Joe said that it looks great. Hope you approve. I think that we are going on strike. If we walk out, could it be when I am in Hawaii so that I don't have to use my sick days? It will be interesting to see how that all plays out. I am not going to "do" Thanksgiving. I can't. Hopefully everyone will understand. If they don't, well I am sorry, but I just can't do it. I know that you understand.

Moll is doing well. That was certainly a quick turnaround regarding the "problem" at her work. How did you do that? Kate just stopped home on her way back from her college reunion. She is doing well, also. Keep on sending the incredible help. We are all MOST APPRECIATIVE of everything that you have done and are doing on our behalf. And the beat goes on and the beat goes on.

It will be fun to see Hawaii again. That plane ride isn't fun though, but it is definitely worth it when you get there. Won't it be great to celebrate Kate's birthday with Paul in Honolulu. YES!! I don't think that I ever wrote that I loved the help in the Waikiki hotel room when I was crying and the movie came on that had Lane Tech High School, where you sometimes worked, in it. That was wild. And then how you resolved everything at Alice's. You are so very dear. I have no idea how you do those PERFECT things. I just keep on saying "that was great, how did you do that, Georgie." I love you.

Remember how I always said "we didn't even know one another when we got married" and you would always say "we knew one another, Betty" and I would say "no, we didn't" and you would say "yes, we did." Well, once again, you were right and how dense was I?! You knew and I understood NOTHING. Didn't that drive you nuts? You were such a gentleman and such a gentle man. And, you still are. I absolutely love you.

I think that's it. I miss you terribly and when I was looking at the one cruise video where you have the life vest on and you start dancing—well, it made me smile and cry at the same time. God, I miss you. Why did I walk through 33 years with my eyes shut? I didn't, did I? It's all your fault. Since you knew, why didn't you shake me and tell me to wake up. It's not really your fault. It's mine. I am now learning my lessons. Just wish that you were standing here so that I could hug you and thank you in person. I do love you, George. Always have and always will.

Have to go to the NPHS Fall Festival. They are going to have puppies and kittens for adoption and Moll wants to check them out. Just what we need. Maybe it is just what we need. Let me know. Be with me, George. I LOVE YOU SOOOOOO MUCH. xo, me

WEDNESDAY, NOVEMBER 5, 2003, 9:50 PM

Oh George,

How did this weekend come about? I really have NO IDEA. It just materialized and I know it is all of your doing. So, not that I want to put any undue pressure on you, BUT do you think that you could do a really, really REALLY HUGE something when everyone is gathered here? It would be too wonderful. You always know how to pull off something subtle, yet unbelievably fantastic and so I am thanking you, in advance, for what ever it is that you have planned. I truly love you and I am very excited about whatever it is that you are going to do.

Some random thoughts: Is this condo the right thing for Kate? Did you help with the job interview for Margaret?

I am so tired, but I am so looking forward to this weekend and to "seeing you." I love you more than I ever dreamed possible.

I trust that you are living with abundance in your heart and in your soul. I am and it's all because of you. I LOVE YOU, George.

oxooxoxoooxoxoxooxoxooxooxoxoxoxooxoxoxox,
Betty

WEDNESDAY, NOVEMBER 5, 2003, 9:57 PM

OK George,

Did you know when you planned this whole get-together that it was going to coincide with the eclipsed moon and the alignment of the 6 planets in the shape of a star?

I know that you planned it that way and I am so excited that I can't quite get my mind straight. I love you and thank you so much for the wild, wonderful ride that you are taking me on. I LOVE IT, but I especially LOVE YOU.

Kisses, kisses, kisses

SUNDAY, NOVEMBER 9, 2003, 11:37 AM

Oh George, I am a bit exhausted. What an experience. Friday was great and the individual sessions with Carol were fantastic. It will take some time to process all that happened and to try to figure out just why this all took place, but it was wonderful. Thank you for doing this for Moll and Jeanine. I love you for everything and for the Astral travels. I KNEW IT!

Love you for eternity, Betty

From Sue
To Betty
Friday, November 14, 2003, 1:27 PM

This reminds me of George, especially the last stanza. Enjoy Hawaii, say Hi to Pele! Enjoy, Sue

I Think Continually of Those Who Were Truly Great
by Stephen Spender

I think of those who were truly great.
Who, from the womb, remembered the soul's history
Through endless corridors of light where the hours are suns,
Endless and singing. Whose lovely ambition
Was that their lips, still touched with fire,
Should tell of the spirit clothed from head to foot in song.
And who hoarded from the spring branches
The desires falling across their bodies like blossoms.

What is precious is never to forget
The delight of the blood drawn from ageless springs
Breaking through rocks in worlds before our earth;
Never to deny its pleasure in the simple morning light,
Nor its grave evening demand for love;
Never to allow gradually the traffic to smother
With noise and fog the flowering of the spirit.
Near the snow, near the sun, in the highest fields

See how these names are feted by the waving grass,
And by the streamers of white cloud,
And whispers of wind in the listening sky;
The names of those who in their lives fought for life,
Who wore at their hearts the fire's center.
Born of the sun they traveled a short while toward the sun,
And left the vivid air signed with their honor.

FRIDAY, NOVEMBER 14, 2003, 10:01 PM

OK Georgie ——————

We're off to Hawaii again. This is really getting to be quite nuts. I simply can't wait to see the ocean. I know that I don't have to invite you, but I need to just say ——- PLEASE be with me and PLEASE give me HUGE, HUGE signs. Continuous huge, huge signs. I am thanking you, in advance, for everything that is going to take place. I can't wait to see what you have in store.

Thank you over and over and over for last weekend with Carol. The full moon and the six planets in the shape of a star—the Harmonic Concordance—WOW! You are pretty good. I always knew that you were/are.

Have to go to bed soon. I am so glad that you are coming with. Let the wild times begin. They already have, thanks to you. I do love you and what's more, I know that you love me. And, I thank you for that. I love you, Georgie. I better get some sleep or else I will be tired tomorrow. Good night.

xoxoxoxoxoxoxoxoxoxoxooxoxxooxxoxx, Betty

WINTER 2003

WEDNESDAY, CHRISTMAS EVE, 2003, 9:30 AM

George,

I am having some difficulty today and I am not certain where it is coming from. I'm feeling rather introspective and somewhat sad. I know that the circumstances of my life are, and always have been, marvelous. Even in adverse situations, I have realized that I am, and will always continue to be, incredibly blessed. And, I am deeply grateful for the gifts of continual/unending blessings.

My "distress," lately, comes from the realization that I don't think that I am giving back to this life proportionally what has been given to me. Maybe it has to do with the vapid, insipid commercialism of this particular time of the year.

When I leave this earth, will I have done anything that contributed to the comfort and happiness of others? Really meaningful contributions. Not simply vacant attempts. Nothing materialistic. Something that reaches another's soul level.

I feel as if I am in some sort of a holding pattern. It is almost as if I am observing my life, while going through the motions. It's a rather unique perspective and somewhat amusing, but never-the-less a little disquieting. The time will come when I am able to act on my ideas. So, I suppose that I should live in the "now," enjoy this time of introspection and simply listen. Maybe this is not a new concept to you, but it is completely foreign to me. Actually, I think that I like this whole experience. Still have no idea where it will lead me, but I'm liking the process. And, what I am manifesting in my thought, I have no doubt but that it will come into being.

Enough of this. It snowed last night. Not much, but I do need to go out and shovel some. It will be interesting, from my new detached perspective, to watch myself do the work. Maybe I won't even get cold.

Take care. Be well. I feel as if I am slowly tumbling backwards into a tunnel and leaving, withdrawing from, all that I have known. Not sure where it will lead to, but I know that it will be just where I am supposed to be. Not frightening. Quite comforting.

Do you think that I am dying? I can't just yet. I still have to do something that will make a difference to someone else in this lifetime.

It is Christmas Eve Day and I wish you a VERY MERRY CHRISTMAS. I have lots of goodies from the Paulina Market for a delicious supper tonight. One of my favorite celebrations. We'll toast to you for old time sake.

I love you from my soul and I am grateful. But, do I miss you? You know that I do.

Love, Betty

THURSDAY, CHRISTMAS DAY, 2003, 9:51 PM

Dear, Dear George,

Merry Christmas to you. How did you celebrate this day? We really had a very nice time of it. This morning, Kate, Moll and I had a delicious breakfast—almost as good as when you did the cooking—and then we opened presents. Then we went to Rita's and had a fun time. I played the piano for the singing and we sang "Rockin' Around The Christmas Tree" about 25 times. It was "over the top" and YES, I did play the one part with my seat, each and every time. Why do I do that? Who knows. It's just fun. That's why. You are so dear and I miss your being where I can see your face and watch you watching the festivities. You were always so good about letting me go a little crazy and never, ever telling me to cut it out or grow up or anything else. I loved you then and I love you now and I will love you forever and I am so grateful and comforted by that knowing. I love you George and if I start crying, I won't stop for a long, long time. So, I can't give in to any sadness. But, please know that I will miss you 'til the moment I take my last breath on this earth. I love you and thank you over and over for being a part of my lifellives. You are my dear, dear Georgie. Merry Christmas.

Love, Betty

WINTER 2004

THURSDAY, NEW YEARS DAY, 2004, 10:22 AM

Well George, it is now 2004. This month marks the second anniversary of your passing. It makes me sort of think of the game "Red Rover, Red Rover, let George come over." I'm happy for you, but NOT for me. These past few days have left me in a state of exhaustion. I didn't realize what was happening to me, but now it is all too clear. The Holiday time, this year, was actually much more difficult than last year. I have no idea what happened, but whatever it was it really took its toll and I have been in bed for two days. Not quite used to doing that.

Thank you a million times over for catapulting the little tree off of the sideboard right in front of Maureen and Nancy. HOW IN THE WORLD (the OUT of this world) DID YOU DO THAT ONE? Pretty impressive I must say. And, thank you, more than you know, for answering my call for help from Carol. When she called, I couldn't believe it. I already knew the message because of my dream, but I can't thank you enough for your help in this matter. God, I love you!! And, thank you for the help with Kate and Moll (condo and medical). No wonder you pulled the pin early. They are going to push me over the edge. No they won't, they are wonderful. Really they are. I love them, BUT... (just kidding)

Take care. HAPPY NEW YEAR to us all. Whatever do you have in store for me this year? I am looking forward to the wild, wild travel adventures. I am sooooooooo thankful that you are my true, true Anam Cara. How would I ever survive this without you? I couldn't/wouldn't.

I love you so very, very much and I am grateful and thankful for your love. I love you, George.

xo, Betty

THURSDAY, JANUARY 8, 2004, 7:28:23 AM

My dear, dear George,

What a wonderful gift to receive from Kris. Her phone call, last night, was a comfort that I had not expected and something that I wouldn't have thought of on my own. Once again, thank you for guiding things in my life that I am unaware of. I love it that she called.

Also, I love it that Carol called the other day. I am really looking forward to the 23rd and the 24th. You are too, too wonderful. You have no idea — well, maybe you do — how much I appreciate your help. It is really quite grand to experience and a delightful wonder to watch things unfold.

I hope that Moll has a great time at her new assignment today and that things go well with Kate's closing on her condo, tomorrow. I know that you will be with us every step of the way. Please give me the thoughts if I miss something. You know that I have come to not only appreciate, but rely on AND expect your help.

This is quite an experience and one that I never dreamed I would be living. I love you, George. But I do not love this cold, cold weather. Some transition has to be done in that area. Hope you think so, too.

Have fun whatever you are doing. I am sorry that we are keeping you so busy with our earthly needs. When you were in your body you were fantastic at being able to do anything. You were such a gentle spirit that I think we wore you out. Now that you are free and able to soar, you are doing a million times more for us. We know it and we are in awe of the possibilities. As that guy that you did electrical work for always said, "Thanks a million."

Have to go to school now. Jeanine is coming for dinner tonight to tell me all about her student teaching experience. "Play the game, Jeanine."

I love you, Georgie. Always have and always will and I am tremendously comforted by that thought.

love, love, love, Betty

WEDNESDAY, JANUARY 21, 2004, 11:07AM

OK George,

Today is the day. It was two years ago that I stood in the street and watched you die.

I love you and that's all I can say at the moment.

xo, Betty

WEDNESDAY, JANUARY 21, 2004, 12:52 PM

George,

As this day progresses, I am having increasing difficulty. I simply refuse to have my emotions ruled by a date on a calendar. If I were in the South of France or on some Caribbean Island it would be different, but I am here in the place where my life forever changed.

209

I suppose that I should ride out the tears, but it is re-upsetting as each wave of sadness washes over me. This is coming out of nowhere and it is totally unexpected. I needed to put it in writing. In a moment, I will be fine. I better be. Maybe I will never be fine. Maybe I never was fine. Whatever.

I just need to remind myself to go within or go without.

Thank you for being.   xo, Betty

WEDNESDAY, JANUARY 21, 2004, 7:22 PM

My Dear, Dear George,

Two years ago, at this very moment, I was standing on the corner of Diversey and Halsted watching the wonderful, glorious life that I knew change instantly and forever. I have survived these two years only because you have made it possible. I can never repay you for the support and tremendous help that you have provided for the three of us. THANK YOU a million times over for all of the bridges that you have built for us. I don't know how this all works, but I am certain that you have other things to be doing besides working overtime for me, Kate and Moll. The sad part is that we came to rely on you when you were here and we still totally rely on you. Have you gotten completely sick of us yet? The truth is that we hope you will never get tired of taking care of us. You must be able to do several things at once, because you certainly have gone above and beyond the call of duty. Kate's condo is FANTASTIC and Moll received a clean bill of health from the Dr. today. So, THANK YOU, THANK YOU, THANK YOU!!

I love you, Georgie. I have no idea what this next year

holds in store, but I am trusting you to keep on keeping on. It will be exciting to see what unfolds. I will miss your beautiful body and your wise, witty, weird words forever. I will miss you 'til the moment I take my last breath. I wouldn't miss you so much if you hadn't been so wonderful and funny. This still is rotten after two years. I feel like saying: "OK, you can come out now." So, I will say it ——- "OK, you can come out now." ... I'm waiting ...

I hope that you are having a wonderful time doing whatever you are doing. I know that you are. I love you dearly. And, I am so very thankful that I love you from my soul, otherwise I would not survive for a moment.

xo, Betty

SUNDAY, FEBRUARY 1, 2004, 10:08 AM

My dear, dear George,

Two years have passed. Two years filled with every emotion imaginable, and then some. How did I get here? I have no idea. I just arrived. Arrived with two questions:

Where did you go?

and

Where am I going?

While I will miss you 'til I take my last breath, I have no choice but to go on and live this life fully. Because of you, I know that wherever I am going, I won't be alone.

I love you, George. Always have and always will. Remember how I repeatedly asked you about the

meaning of the last line in the poem "Time" ————
"and for those who love, time is eternity." You would patiently explain it over and over and over and I would forget and ask you again and again and again. Well, I now understand it completely. Until we meet again, I thank you for, and am eternally grateful for, that love.

You are my Anam Cara.

Peace and Joy and Love and Gratitude, Betty

THE FINAL COMMUNICATION

I had reached the end of my e-mails to George, but, four months later, I felt the need to send another. Below is my second-to-last message.

TUESDAY, MAY 18, 2004, 5:01 PM

> *I just wanted to let you know that I love you soooooooooooooo much!!! AND, I thank you for everything and I miss you terribly!!*
>
> *LOVE, Betty*

Each time when I had written to George, I would type out the message, hit SEND and then PRINT. Like clockwork, my method never failed; never failed, that is, until my very *last* message.

On the following day, May 19, I wrote George a final e-mail.

When I hit PRINT, two pages came out; two pages that I hadn't written.

But I know who did write them ...

The messages were loud and clear and I know that they were heaven sent.

WEDNESDAY, MAY 19, 2004, 5:01 PM

PAGE ONE:

[symbolic/pictographic message]

PAGE TWO:

? n♥ n? L ■■ ●L■ ? ♥ n ? ?
n♥ nüüü91w≤n L? L n ☉Ln ☉Ln ☉Ln L♥ .Lon

n?² ●L■ L ?■ ≡ ≡ ≡üüü105w·● n²≡ ≡? ■●♀

I've tried to crack this code several times without success. I have no clue as to what these symbols say. I don't even remember what it was that I had written to generate this unusual print. All I know is that it is the most beautiful writing I have ever received.

I love it! I absolutely love it!

Once again, I simply had to say "Thank You."

ABOUT THE AUTHOR

BETTY WALDRON PORTENLANGER is a life-long Chicagoan. With the exception of a very brief stint on the Chicago Police Force, her life's work has been with the Chicago Board of Education, as a kindergarten teacher. Five-year-old children hold a special place in her heart. Now retired, Betty considers it a privilege to have been able to work with children and their families.

It is her hope that this account of an extremely personal and private experience will be of benefit to others.

Upon completion of her writing, Betty reflected: "I would be lightened if I knew that, by sharing these stories, I had helped another on his or her own way."

ISBN 141205751-5